Please Pass the Potatoes

a Appezling Recipes

from the Society of St. Andrew

St. Andrew Press
Big Island, Virginia

Please Pass the Potatoes
a Appealing Recipes

from the Society of St. Andrew

Copyright 1990 by St. Andrew Press

Front cover design: Alfons J. Beisser

First Printing, September 1990

Library of Congress Cataloging-in-Publication Data

Please pass the potatoes: appealing recipes/from the Society of St. Andrew.

       p.   cm.
   ISBN 0-939485-07-9 : $7.50
   1. Cookery (Potatoes)   I. Society of St. Andrew.
TX803.P8P54   1990   90-9033
  641.6'521--dc20   CIP

ISBN 0-939485-07-9

Introduction

Since the inception of the Potato Project in 1983, the phrase "please pass the potatoes" has been attached to the program. Our job is to see that potatoes are "passed" to the hungry of our nation.

These potatoes may be ugly, misshapen, nicked, too small, or even too large for market. Over 95 million pounds of potatoes and other produce that do not meet market standards have been passed to the hungry through food banks, soup kitchens, inner city ministries, Salvation Armies, and Native American Reservations. That translates into almost 300 million servings of potatoes that have been passed to the hungry in the past seven years.

Almost since the first shipment of potatoes was delivered, a potato cookbook has been one of our dreams. With a great deal of help and encouragement from our friends, the dream is now a reality. We hope as you read these pages you will not only find recipes that you enjoy for years to come, but that you will learn a little more about the Society of St. Andrew and its exciting ministries on behalf of the hungry.

It really doesn't matter whether you use pretty potatoes or ugly potatoes in these recipes, the taste will be the same. However, by your purchase of **PLEASE PASS THE POTATOES**, you have helped to "pass potatoes" to others who may have nothing but a potato for their next meal. All the profits from **PLEASE PASS THE POTATOES** go to feeding the hungry.

"PLEASE PASS THE POTATOES" is dedicated to Bill Schminkey of Fairlington United Methodist Church in Alexandria, VA. Bill's commitment to the hungry and his efforts on behalf of the Potato Project have been and continue to be an inspiration to all of us.

Bill, with the support of Fairlington UMC, started the St. Andrew Club in 1986. Since then over $250,000 has been raised resulting in the distribution of over 7.5 million pounds of potatoes to the hungry of our country. We are deeply thankful for Bill's leadership and the participation of each of the St. Andrew Club members. Without the concern and support of these individuals much produce would have needlessly gone to waste and many would have remained hungry.

If you are interested in more information regarding the St. Andrew Club or in becoming a member please write:

> Bill Schminkey
> St. Andrew Club
> 3900 King Street
> Alexandria, VA 22302

We at the Society of St. Andrew wish to express our appreciation to all those who donated recipes for **PLEASE PASS THE POTATOES**, especially to the members of the St. Andrew Club. Without the recipes there would be no cookbook. We also deeply appreciate the hard work of Sharon Kourtz in the early stages of preparing the manuscript.

We discovered that there are many wonderful cooks out there. Enjoy their recipes! We regret that not all the recipes we received made it into print. Because of space limitations we were forced to exclude duplications. When you try these wonderful ways of preparing the "old favorite", each of you should expect to hear the phrase we have come to love:

"Please pass the potatoes!"

> Very special thanks go to Jean Horne, Susan Allen, Jeff Allen, Ken Horne, Susan Clark, Ann Goff, David Horne, and Mitchell Bond for all the their efforts in the completion of our cookbook. They were a tremendous help.

TABLE OF CONTENTS

notes

6

The Society of St. Andrew

The Society of St. Andrew, began as a church affiliated community in 1979, and was incorporated as a private, nonprofit, tax-exempt organization in 1983. From our inception, we have had a vision of a world without hunger. All our efforts have been aimed at transforming that vision into a reality during our lifetime.

Even though hunger is an immense tragedy that impacts the lives of untold millions, we have learned that one person can make a difference on behalf of the hungry. If each of us would become involved, and do what we could as individuals, our united efforts could erase the obscenity of hunger.

"Please pass the potatoes" is a phrase that rolls off the tongue. For some of us it is a phrase we hear almost every day. We would encourage each of those reading this cookbook to make a conscious effort to do something for the hungry. Get involved. Small steps are important. You can make a difference. Join the Society of St. Andrew in our efforts to end hunger in our lifetime.

POTATO PROJECT

In a country like ours, that produces food in abundance, there is no need for anyone to go hungry. Each year we in the United States waste more than enough food to feed all our poor and hungry citizens. The Potato Project, begun in June 1983, has salvaged and distributed over 95 million pounds of potatoes and other vegetables that otherwise would have been thrown out to rot. This food, valued at well over $6,500,000.00 has been delivered to agencies that serve the poor at a cost of less than four cents per pound.

Hundreds of agencies in every state in the Union have been organized to distribute food to the poor. Potatoes and other produce that is salvageable in truckload size lots (45,000 pounds each) are grown in widespread but geographically localized areas. The Potato Project serves as the indispensable conduit between those who have produce that will be needlessly wasted and those who can distribute that produce to the needy.

If there were no Potato Project millions of pounds of food would be needlessly wasted each year and thousands would go hungry while good food rotted away. The Potato Project helps to fight this obscenity. The amount of produce that is salvaged and delivered each year is limited only by our financial ability to cover the four cents per pound necessary to bag and ship the donated produce.

HARVEST OF HOPE

In 1985, we saw the need to educate our youth about the realities of hunger and waste and to provide them a hands-on opportunity to put that education into action. The Harvest of Hope, begun in July 1985, has involved over 1400 young people from 11 states. They have studied hunger, the need to conserve our resources, biblical teachings about the poor, and all the related issues that, when resolved, can make a world without hunger possible. They have also worked hard in fields of tomatoes, peppers, corn, and dozens of other vegetables that would not be harvested otherwise. Tons of vegetables have been delivered to the poor by Harvest of Hope participants. Many people have been touched by the Harvest of Hope ministry.

The Harvest of Hope gives its participants the opportunity to do something about hunger. Food that would otherwise be left in the field to rot is saved and given to the poor, but much more than this is accomplished.

Matching hard physical labor with intensive study gives the participants a chance to look at themselves. They are able to see the relationship between youth, lifestyles, and values, and how these fit together. For many of the participants, Harvest of Hope marks the beginning of a long-term commitment to finding a way to end hunger in our world.

If hunger is to be overcome in our time, it will be done by people like our Harvest of Hopers who see the need and make the commitment. Inspiring young people in this way is the most important investment we can make in our future. Harvest of Hope is pleased to have been able to do so much in the past. We look forward to a greatly expanded program in the future.

GLEANING NETWORK

Drawing on our experience in the Harvest of Hope, we saw the possibility of organizing farmers, volunteers and small-scale food distributors so that food left in the fields after harvest could be gleaned and given to the poor locally. The Gleaning Network, begun in Virginia in 1988, has involved over 1,500 volunteers in gleaning and distributing over 800,000 pounds of produce to local feeding agencies. It is possible to establish this network all across the nation, involving thousands of volunteers and salvaging millions of pounds of food.

The Gleaning Network acts as a clearinghouse whose task is to connect farmers with gleanable produce, volunteers willing to glean, and agencies that provide food to the hungry. Our staff recruits farmers who have crops that are sometimes not harvested for market imposed reasons. These farmers agree to call us when they have produce to glean. Our staff then recruits volunteers in that area to glean on a stand-by basis. We also locate the nearest food distribution agency and secure a commitment to take the gleaned produce and distribute it to the poor.

When a farmer does call with gleanable produce our staff alerts the volunteers and the distribution agency. The food is gleaned, delivered and distributed to the poor. In most cases this takes place in or near the locality where the food is grown. In this way we have created an opportunity for local people to help the poor while fighting waste in their own community.

The Gleaning Network operates on a regional basis. Thus far the program is active in Virginia, Maryland, North Carolina, and Washington, D.C. However, it is possible to duplicate this program across our nation! Literally thousands of farmers and volunteers could be involved and tens of millions of pounds of food salvaged for the poor.

INTERNATIONAL PROGRAM

Although the Society of St. Andrew has primarily focused on the need to alleviate hunger and waste within the United States, we do recognize the need to reach beyond our borders. In 1985, we worked with Church World Service to ship potatoes to the Dominican Republic where they were distributed to Haitian refugees during the crisis in that country. In 1986, we responded to the earthquake in Mexico City by sending potatoes to victims of that tragedy. In 1987, we began a pilot project of supplying seed potatoes to farmers in the mountains of Jamaica where an extensive banana blight has contributed to an unemployment rate that continues to exceed ninety percent. In 1988, we began an ongoing involvement with the construction and completion of an agricultural training school in Kenya. Kenya is one of many third world countries where agricultural techniques and practices must be improved in order to avoid future famines.

Our international experience has shown us that we can have our greatest impact, not in the project and program development area where many competent agencies are active, but in the area of communication and coordination. We are active overseas primarily in three ways. We are ready and willing to continue to respond to disasters where our expertise and resources can be useful. We are engaged in promoting deserving projects of local origin that have a hard time promoting themselves in this country. And finally, we see a great need and opportunity to serve as a clearinghouse for groups, agencies and projects that could benefit each other but who seldom have any mutual contact. This last emphasis is extremely important. Resources in the third world are so scarce and the need is so great that any kind of waste (of time, money, talent, duplication of effort and so on) is simply unacceptable. We will continue to work toward eliminating hunger overseas by connecting relief and development efforts to the benefit of all.

SUPPORTING SERVICES

Funding for our various hunger ministries comes from a variety of sources. We are fortunate to receive contributions from a great many churches, foundations, church agencies, corporations and private individuals across the nation. As befits a "product supplying" agency, most of our funding comes from church congregations and individuals. These two sources supply funds on an ongoing basis (as opposed to seed money) and they are a constantly growing portion of our funding base.

Because churches are such an important part of our hunger work and because the teachings of the Bible form the basic rationale behind all we do, the Society of St. Andrew carries on small publishing and teaching operations. The St. Andrew Press publishes materials on hunger and related subjects that are used by churches in the promotion of our hunger work. Some of our staff are also available for leading spiritual life retreats for those who wish to explore futher the area of their interaction with God and the poor.

Salads

notes

CONFETTI POTATO SALAD

6 medium potatoes, cubed
1/4 c. lemon juice
2 medium onions, sliced
6 hard-cooked eggs, quartered
1 medium green pepper, diced
1/4 c. pimento, diced
1 Tbsp. salt
Dash pepper
1/4 c. low-calorie mayonnaise-type salad dressing

Cook potatoes in lightly salted water to which 2 Tbsp. lemon juice have been added for 15 minutes, or until just tender; drain. In large serving bowl, combine hot potatoes and remaining ingredients. Toss gently. Refrigerate to chill.

Yield: 12 servings

CAESAR POTATO SALAD

1 egg
1/4 c. low-calorie Italian dressing
1/4 c. grated Romano cheese
1 Tbsp. Worcestershire sauce
2 tsp. prepared mustard
1 tsp. salt
4 medium potatoes, peeled, cooked and cubed
4 pitted ripe olives, sliced

In large bowl, with wire whisk, beat together egg, Italian dressing, cheese, Worcestershire sauce, mustard and salt until well blended. Add potatoes and olives; toss to mix well. Refrigerate to chill.

Yield: 8 servings

HOT GERMAN POTATO SALAD

1 can (10 3/4 oz.) condensed cream of celery soup
2 Tbsp. lemon juice
4 medium potatoes, peeled, cooked and cubed
1/2 c. celery, sliced
1/4 c. parsley, chopped
2 tsp. salt
1/2 tsp. sugar
dash pepper
1 Tbsp. bacon-flavored bits

In large saucepan, combine soup, lemon juice and 1/4 cup water. Heat, stirring occasionally. Stir in remaining ingredients except bacon bits. Cook just until heated through, stirring constantly and gently. Serve immediately topped with bacon bits.

Yield: 8 servings

PINK POTATO SALAD

3/4 c. low-fat cottage cheese
3 Tbsp. low-calorie French dressing
1 Tbsp. wine vinegar
1 tsp. salt
1 tsp. paprika
dash pepper
4 c. potatoes, cooked and cubed
1 c. celery, sliced
1/4 c. pimento, chopped

In electric blender, combine cottage cheese, French dressing, wine vinegar, salt, paprika and pepper until fairly smooth. In large bowl, combine potatoes, celery and pimento. Toss with cottage cheese mixture. Chill.

Yield: 10 servings

STUFFED TOMATO-POTATO SALAD

4 large tomatoes
1 medium potato, peeled, cooked and diced
1 medium carrot, peeled and chopped
1/4 c. low-fat cottage cheese
2 Tbsp. parsley, chopped
1/2 tsp. salt

Cut tomatoes in halves; scoop out centers to make cups. Strain pulp to remove excess liquid; reserve pulp. Pat insides of tomato cups with paper towels to dry. Combine reserved tomato pulp, potato, carrot, cottage cheese, parsley and salt. Spoon mixture into tomato cups; chill.

Yield: 8 stuffed tomatoes

SALMON POTATO SALAD

4 medium potatoes, washed, cooked, peeled, and diced (4 c.)
1 can (16 oz.) red salmon, drained and flaked
2 c. celery, minced
1/2 c. green onions, chopped
1 envelope unflavored gelatin
2 Tbsp. lemon juice
1/4 c. boiling water
1 1/2 c. mayonnaise
1 tsp. salt
1/4 tsp. cayenne pepper
cherry tomatoes (optional)

Lightly oil a 6-cup ring-mold or bowl; set aside. Combine potatoes, salmon, celery, and onions in large bowl. Combine gelatin and lemon juice in small bowl; let stand 5 minutes to soften gelatin. Add boiling water; stir to dissolve. Stir in mayonnaise, salt, and cayenne; blend well. Pour over potato mixture; toss to coat evenly. Spoon evenly into prepared ring mold. Chill at least 1 hour. Unmold onto serving plate. Fill center of ring with cherry tomatoes.

Yield: 6 servings

SKILLET SUPPER SALAD

5 slices bacon
1 medium onion, chopped
3/4 c. celery, sliced
6 frankfurters, cut diagonally into 1/2-inch slices
1 1/2 Tbsp. all-purpose flour
1/3 c. vinegar
1 tsp. salt
1/4 tsp. pepper
2 tsp. sugar
1 Tbsp. prepared mustard
4 c. potatoes, cooked, peeled and sliced
1/2 tsp. celery seed
3/4 c. water

Fry bacon in large skillet until crisp. Remove bacon with slotted spoon; drain on paper towels. Crumble; set aside. Add onion and celery to drippings in skillet; sauté until onion is transparent. Remove with slotted spoon to small bowl; set aside. Add frankfurters to drippings in skillet; brown on all sides; remove with slotted spoon to small bowl. Stir flour, vinegar, salt, pepper, and 3/4 cup water into drippings in skillet. Cook on moderate heat, stirring constantly until thickened. Stir in sugar and mustard. Add potatoes, frankfurters, onion mixture, and celery seed; stir just to combine. Simmer 10 minutes. Sprinkle bacon on top before serving.

Yield: 6 servings

Potatoes can be dressed up or down. Here are some ways to fix potatoes. They can be baked, boiled, broiled, canned, chipped, creamed, made into croquettes, cubed, flaked, fried, frittered, grated, hash browned, mashed, and they can be made into pancakes and into salads.

NICOISE SALAD

1/4 c. red wine vinegar
3/4 c. olive or vegetable oil
2 Tbsp. green onion, chopped
2 Tbsp. parsley, minced
1 tsp. dry mustard
1 1/4 tsp. salt, divided
1/8 tsp. pepper
4 large potatoes, washed; do not peel
ice water
1 lb. green beans, trimmed
1 head Boston lettuce
1 can (7 oz.) tuna, drained and flaked
3 large tomatoes, peeled and quartered
3 hard-cooked eggs, quartered
1 can (2 oz.) flat anchovy fillets, drained
1/2 c. pitted ripe olives, quartered
1 Tbsp. capers

Combine vinegar, oil, green onion, parsley, mustard, 1/4 teaspoon salt, and pepper in pint jar. Cover, shake to blend, set aside. Bring water and 1 teaspoon salt to a boil in large saucepan. Add potatoes; cover and boil 20 minutes, or until tender; drain. Plunge into ice water; drain. Peel and slice potatoes. Place in large bowl. Shake dressing; pour enough dressing over sliced potatoes just to coat; mix gently. Cover and refrigerate at least 2 hours. Cut beans into 1 1/2-inch pieces. Cook beans in boiling salted water to cover, 7 to 10 minutes, or until crisp-tender; drain. Plunge into ice water; drain. Pour enough dressing over beans just to coat. Cover and refrigerate until chilled. To serve, mound potatoes in center of lettuce-lined platter. Arrange tuna on top of potatoes. Alternately arrange beans, tomato, and eggs around edge of platter. Arrange anchovy fillets on top of beans. Garnish with capers and olives. Pour the remaining dressing over all.

Yield: 6 servings

CALICO SALAD

1 pkg. (10 oz.) frozen mixed vegetables, cooked according to
  package instructions
1 large green pepper, seeded and diced
1 c. celery, sliced thinly
1 large potato, washed, cooked, peeled and cubed
1 small onion, chopped
1 can (15 oz.) red kidney beans, drained
1/4 c. parsley, minced
1/2 c. sugar
3 Tbsp. all-purpose flour
5 tsp. prepared mustard
1/2 c. cider vinegar

Combine mixed vegetables, green pepper, celery, potato, onion,
kidney beans, and parsley in a large bowl; cover and refrigerate.
Combine sugar, flour, mustard, and vinegar in small saucepan.
Cook on moderate heat, stirring constantly, until mixture thick-
ens. Remove from heat; set aside to cool. Pour over vegetables.
Do not mix. Cover and refrigerate at least 8 hours or overnight.

Yield: 6 servings

SUPERB GARDEN SALAD

1 c. whole green beans (trimmed)
4 medium potatoes, washed, cooked, peeled, and diced (4 cups)
2 tomatoes, cut into wedges
10 radishes, sliced
1/2 cucumber, peeled and sliced
10 green onions, cut into 1/2-inch pieces
4 c. lettuce, romaine, and endive (mixed)
1 c. Italian dressing

Cook green beans in water until crisp-tender; drain. Plunge into
ice water; let stand until cool; drain. Combine potatoes, beans,
tomatoes, radishes, cucumber, green onions, and salad greens in
large salad bowl. Slowly pour on salad dressing. Toss slightly to
mix. Serve immediately.

Yield: 6 servings

POTATO SALAD

2 c. potatoes, cooked and diced
1/4 c. green pepper, sliced
1/4 c. onion, diced
1 tsp. celery seed
1/2 c. mayonnaise
1/4 c. mustard
salt and pepper

Drain potatoes and cool. Add onion and green pepper while hot. When cool add mustard, celery seed, mayonnaise, and salt and pepper to taste.

Sauce:

2 eggs
1 c. sugar
1/4 c. vinegar
1/2 stick butter

Beat eggs; add sugar and vinegar. Cook about 10 minutes. Add butter, cook till melted. Cool and add to potatoes.

Yield: 4-6 servings

Debbie W. Horne
Natural Bridge, VA

> 'We are the world,
> We are the children,
> We are the ones
>   who make a brighter day,
> So, let's start giving.'
> -Michael Jackson & Lionel Richie

HOT FRANK POTATO SALAD

1/2 lb. bacon
3/4 c. onion, chopped
3 Tbsp. sugar
3 Tbsp. flour
1 1/2 tsp. salt
1 tsp. celery seed
3/4 c. cider vinegar
1 1/2 c. water
6 c. potatoes, sliced and cooked
8 frankfurters, sliced
2 hard cooked eggs, chopped
chopped parsley

Fry bacon until crisp; drain and crumble; sauté onion in 1/3 c. bacon drippings until tender. Add next 4 ingredients. Stir in vinegar and water. Cook until thick. Combine with bacon, potatoes, frankfurters and eggs. Turn into greased 3-qt. casserole. Bake, covered at 350 degrees for 20 minutes or until heated through. Garnish with parsley.

Yield: 8 large servings

Mrs. Roland Holmes
Pittsburgh, KS

APPLE-POTATO SALAD

6 medium potatoes, washed, cooked, and sliced (about 6 cups)
2 c. red apples, thinly sliced
1 c. celery, diced
1/2 c. green pepper, diced
1/4 c. onion, minced
1 c. dairy sour cream or plain yogurt
1/2 c. mayonnaise
1 tsp. salt
1/4 tsp. celery seed
dash pepper
mixed salad greens
1/4 c. walnuts or pecans, coarsely chopped

Combine potatoes, apples, celery, green pepper, and onion in large bowl. Combine sour cream, mayonnaise, salt, celery seed, and pepper in small bowl; blend well. Stir into potato mixture; blend well. Cover and chill several hours to blend flavors. Arrange salad greens in large salad bowl or on individual plates. Spoon potato salad on top. Sprinkle with nuts.

Yield: 8 servings

DOT'S POTATO SALAD

4 c. mayonnaise
1/2 c. cider vinegar
2 Tbsp. sugar
2 Tbsp. salt
1 tsp. pepper
7 lbs. potatoes, cooked, peeled and cut into bite-size pieces
4 c. celery, chopped
1 doz. hard boiled eggs, chopped (optional)
1 large onion, chopped
1 c. parsley, chopped (fresh is preferred)

In large bowl, with wire whisk or spoon, combine the first five ingredients. Then stir in potatoes, celery, eggs, onion, and parsley. Mix. Cover and refrigerate.

Yield: 24 servings

Dorothy Schminkey
Arlington, VA

PARTY HAM AND POTATO SALAD

9 slices boiled ham, divided
1 envelope unflavored gelatin
2 tsp. cider vinegar
1/3 c. boiling water
3/4 c. mayonnaise
1 tsp. prepared mustard
2 tsp. onion, minced
6 medium potatoes, washed, cooked, and diced
1/2 c. celery, thinly sliced
1/4 c. green pepper, minced
1 jar (2 oz.) pimento, drained and diced
3 hard-cooked eggs, sliced
1 head Boston lettuce

Line 9 X 5-inch loaf pan with 2 strips wax paper — 1 lengthwise, 1 crosswise. Line pan with 3 ham slices, covering bottom and sides completely. Mince 5 ham slices; set aside. Combine gelatin and vinegar in small bowl; let stand 5 minutes to soften. Add boiling water; stir to dissolve gelatin. Combine mayonnaise, mustard, onion, and gelatin in large bowl; blend well. Stir in potatoes, celery, green pepper, minced ham, pimento, and all but 5 egg slices; stir gently to blend. Pour into prepared loaf pan; press lightly to smooth top. Cover with remaining ham slice. Cover pan with plastic wrap; refrigerate 1 hour, or until set. To serve, turn out onto lettuce-lined platter; peel and discard wax paper. Garnish with reserved egg slices. Slice to serve.

Yield: 8 servings

MOLDED CHICKEN & POTATO SALAD

1 3 lb. broiler-fryer
1 medium onion
water
4 medium potatoes (1 1/2 lb.)
1 10-oz. pkg. frozen peas & carrots
3 Tbsp. milk
2 Tbsp. lemon juice
1 1/2 tsp. salt
1/4 tsp. pepper
mayonnaise

2 medium celery stalks, thinly sliced
1 large carrot for garnish
1 green onion for garnish

About 5 1/2 hours before serving or day ahead:

Rinse chicken, its giblets and neck with running cold water.
Place chicken, breast-side down, in saucepan or saucepot just
large enough to hold the chicken (4- to 5-quart size). Add giblets,
neck, onion, and 2 inches water; over high heat, heat to boiling.
Reduce heat to low, cover, and simmer 35 minutes or until
chicken is fork-tender. Remove chicken, giblets, and neck to
large bowl; refrigerate 30 minutes or until easy to handle.
(Refrigerate or freeze chicken broth to use in soup another day.)

Meanwhile, in 3-quart saucepan over high heat, heat potatoes
and enough water to cover and bring to boiling. Reduce heat to
medium-low; cover and cook 25 to 30 minutes until potatoes are
fork-tender. Drain potatoes. Cool potatoes until easy to handle;
peel and dice. In same saucepan, prepare frozen peas and carrots as label directs; drain.

When chicken is cool, discard skin and bones; cut meat and
giblets into small pieces. In large bowl, mix milk, lemon juice,
salt, pepper, and 3/4 c. mayonnaise until blended. Add chicken,
potatoes, peas and carrots, celery; toss to coat well with dressing.

Line 2 1/2-qt. bowl with plastic wrap; spoon chicken salad
mixture into lined bowl, packing it well. Cover and refrigerate
until well chilled, about 3 hours.

To Serve Molded Chicken & Potato Salad:

Invert salad onto platter. Spread 1/2 c. mayonnaise over out-
side of salad. For garnish, cut carrot into thin slices. If you
like, with flower shaped canape cutter, cut carrot slices into
flowers. Dip green onion into very hot water for a few seconds;
drain; cut into pieces for stems and leaves. Arrange carrot and
green onion on molded salad to make an attractive design.

Yield: 6 large servings

POTATO BEAN SALAD

6 medium-size potatoes, cooked and diced
1 c. whole dill pickles, chopped
1/2 c. onion, chopped
1/2 c. mayonnaise or salad dressing
1 can (16 oz.) barbecue beans
salt

Toss potatoes, pickles, and onion in large bowl. Mix beans with
mayonnaise or salad dressing and pour over potato mixture.
Toss gently until all ingredients are well blended. Chill well.

Yield: 6-8 servings

R. Babcock
Lynchburg, VA

POTATO SALAD ROMANO

3 lbs. small red potatoes, washed
ice water
1/2 lb. Swiss cheese, cut into 2 X 1/8-inch strips
1 1/2 c. mayonnaise
1 tsp. chives, minced
3/4 tsp. salt
1/4 tsp. cayenne pepper
1/4 lb. cooked ham, diced
2 large fresh mushrooms, sliced

Place potatoes in large saucepan; add water to cover. Bring to a
boil; cover and simmer 20 minutes, or until tender; drain.
Plunge into ice water; let stand until cool enough to handle;
drain. Peel and thinly slice potatoes. Combine potatoes and
cheese in large bowl. Combine mayonnaise, chives, salt, and
cayenne in separate bowl; blend well. Spoon mayonnaise mix-

ture over potatoes and cheese; stir gently to coat. Cover and refrigerate at least 5 to 6 hours. Sprinkle with ham.

Yield: 6 servings

MOMMA'S POTATO SALAD FOR A CROWD

5 lbs. potatoes (washed and peeled or unpeeled if you prefer)

Cut the potatoes in bite-size pieces, cover with water and boil 10-15 min., or until done. Drain and sprinkle with vinegar. Toss with dressing.

Dressing:

3 c. salad-dressing type mayonnaise
1/2 c. apple cider vinegar, approximately
1/2 tsp. salt
1/2 tsp. pepper
2 Tbsp. sugar (optional)
1 Tbsp. prepared mustard
1 large onion, chopped
2 large celery stalks, chopped
2 tsp. celery seed

Mix mayonnaise with spices, then add vinegar until desired consistency. Toss with potatoes. Sprinkle with additional celery seed. Serve immediately warm, or refrigerate several hours to blend flavors. It is really better the second day.

Yield: 20 servings

Jean K. Horne
Bedford, VA

SWEET POTATO SALAD

4 large unpared, cored Red Delicious apples cut into 1/2-inch
  chunks
2 c. celery, chopped
1/2 c. raisins
1/2 c. walnuts, coarsely chopped
1 can (1 lb.) sweet potatoes, chilled, well drained and diced
1 c. sour cream
salt
1 Tbsp. milk

Combine apples, celery, raisins, walnuts with sour cream.
Gently fold in diced sweet potatoes. Cover and refrigerate until
ready to serve.

Yield: 6-8 servings

PINEAPPLE SWEET POTATO SALAD

1 can pineapple tidbits, drained
3 c. cooked sweet potatoes, cubed
2 Tbsp. lemon juice
2 Tbsp. pineapple syrup
salt to taste
1 tsp. sugar
1/4 tsp. onion salt
1/4 tsp. nutmeg
3/4 c. celery, sliced
2 Tbsp. green pepper or pimento, chopped
2 Tbsp. sliced almonds

Mix together first 7 ingredients and pour over potatoes.   Mix
well. Let stand for several hours. Add remaining ingredients;
toss slightly. Serve on bed of lettuce leaves.

Yield: 6 servings

BEEFY POTATO SALAD

1 lb. lean beef round, cooked (well-trimmed)
3 Tbsp. wine vinegar
1 Tbsp. ketchup
1/2 tsp. prepared mustard
2 medium potatoes, peeled, cooked and cubed
1/4 c. fresh mushrooms, sliced
1/4 c. yogurt
lettuce leaves

Cut beef into 1/2-inch cubes. In large bowl, combine beef, vinegar, ketchup and mustard; marinate for two hours in refrigerator, stirring occasionally. Add potatoes, mushrooms and yogurt. Toss gently to mix well. Chill. Serve on lettuce leaves.

Yield: 4 servings

RED-ONION POTATO SALAD

6 medium potatoes, peeled, cooked and sliced
1 c. celery, sliced
1 c. red onion, thinly sliced
1/3 c. parsley, chopped
1/4 c. low calorie Italian dressing
3 Tbsp. wine vinegar
2 tsp. salt
dash cayenne pepper

In large bowl, combine hot potatoes with remaining ingredients. Refrigerate to chill.

Yield: 6 servings

GRANDMOTHER O'BRYANT'S POTATO SALAD

4-6 potatoes (depending on size)
2 large eggs
1 small onion
1/4 c. mayonnaise (more or less to taste)
2 Tbsp. vinegar (more or less to taste)
1 tsp. salt (more or less to taste)
pinch garlic

Boil potatoes until cooked; mash thoroughly. Hard boil the
eggs; set aside to cool. Chop onion into very fine pieces.
Separate egg whites from yolks; chop whites into small pieces.
In mixing or serving bowl combine mashed potatoes, onion, egg
whites, mayonnaise, vinegar and salt. Mix thoroughly. Form
potato mixture into pleasing shape in bowl; grate the egg yolks
on top of potato mixture. If desired, garlic may be added to potatoes or used to rub the mixing bowl before preparing.

Yield: 4-6 servings

Fred O'Bryant
Charlottesville, VA

Nutritional Info Per Serving

Serving size: One medium potato
   (150 grams)   about 1/3 pound
Calories..110
Protein................................3 grams
Carbohydrates................23 grams
Fat...0 grams
Dietary fiber...................2710 mg.
Sodium...................................10 mg.
Potassium...........................750 mg.

Soups

notes

CREAM OF POTATO SOUP FOR HEART PATIENTS

4 Tbsp. corn oil margarine
1 c. onion, chopped
1/2 c. celery, chopped
3 c. potatoes, diced
2 c. low sodium chicken broth
1/2 c. fresh parsley, chopped
1/2 tsp. thyme, crushed
1/2 tsp. celery seed
1/2 tsp. salt (if desired)
1/4 tsp. pepper
3 c. skim milk

In medium saucepan over medium high heat melt margarine, add onion and celery and cook 4 minutes, or until soft, stirring frequently. Add potatoes, chicken broth, parsley, thyme, celery seed, salt and pepper. Bring to boil, reduce heat, and cover. Simmer about 15 minutes or until potatoes are almost tender. Add milk, simmer uncovered about 5 minutes, stirring occasionally. In blender at medium speed, blend about 1/4 of the mixture at a time until smooth. Return to saucepan and heat about 1 minute.

Yield: 8-10 servings

Katherine H. Vincent
Lynchburg, VA

LADY ALLEN'S POTATO SOUP

6 chicken bouillon cubes
6 c. water
3 c. potatoes, sliced
3 c. onions, sliced
1 c. whipping cream or half-and-half

Cook potatoes and onions in the water with bouillon cubes until tender. Let cool. Put in blender about 2 minutes. Add cream. Reheat before serving.

Yield: 4-6 servings

Selene Stewart
Lynchburg, VA

POTATO-SAUSAGE SOUP

1 lb. sausage
2 c. onions, chopped
1 c. celery, chopped
3 c. water
2 cubes chicken bouillon
1/4 tsp. garlic powder
2 tsp. salt
pepper to taste
1/4 tsp. thyme
6-7 potatoes, medium size, cubed
3 c. milk

In medium saucepan cook sausage, onions, and celery until meat is brown and vegetables are tender. Drain off any fat. Add water, chicken bouillon, and seasonings. Stir in potatoes and cook until tender. Mash potatoes slightly. Stir in milk and heat to serving temperature.

Yield: 8-10 servings

Mrs. Becky Gwaltney
Smithfield, VA

HAM AND POTATO CHOWDER

2 Tbsp. butter or margarine
1/2 c. onion, chopped
1/4 c. green pepper, chopped
4 medium potatoes, washed, peeled and cubed (3 cups)
1 tsp. salt
1/4 tsp. paprika
1/8 tsp. pepper
3 Tbsp. all-purpose flour
2 c. milk
1 can (12 oz.) whole-kernel corn, drained
1 1/2 c. cooked ham, diced

Melt butter in 3 1/2-quart saucepan. Sauté onion and green pepper until tender. Add potatoes, 2 cups water, salt, paprika, and pepper. Cover and simmer about 15 minutes, or until potatoes are tender. Combine flour and 1/3 cup water in small bowl; blend well. Stir into potato mixture. Add milk. Simmer until slightly thickened, stirring frequently. Add corn and ham; heat through.

Yield: 6 servings

> *'Pray for peace and grace and spiritual food,*
> *For wisdom and guidance, for all these are good,*
> *But don't forget the potatoes'.*
> *-John Tyler Pettee*

AUTUMN SOUP

1 lb. lean ground beef
1 c. onion, chopped
2 c. potatoes, washed and diced
1 1/2 c. carrots, thinly sliced
1 c. celery, diced
3 beef bouillon cubes
1 clove garlic, minced
1 tsp. salad herbs
1 bay leaf
1 tsp. salt
1/4 tsp. pepper
6 tomatoes, peeled and chopped

Brown beef in large saucepan, stirring to break up beef. Add onions; cook 5 minutes. Drain fat. Add 2 quarts water, potatoes, carrots, celery, bouillon, garlic, salad herbs, bay leaf, salt, and pepper. Bring to a boil; cover and simmer 30 minutes, or until vegetables are tender. Add tomatoes; cover and simmer 10 minutes. Discard bay leaf.

Yield: 8 servings

POTATO CHOWDER

2 slices bacon, cut into 1/2-inch pieces
1 medium onion, chopped
2 1/2 c. potatoes, washed and diced into 1/2-inch pieces
3/4 c. carrots, thinly sliced
2 c. boiling water
1 tsp. salt
3/4 tsp. parsley flakes
1/4 tsp. sage
1/4 tsp. paprika
1/8 tsp. white pepper
3 c. milk, divided
3 Tbsp. all-purpose flour

Fry bacon in 3 1/2-quart saucepan until crisp. Remove bacon with slotted spoon; drain on paper towels. Crumble bacon; set aside. Add onion to drippings in saucepan; cook until transparent. Add potatoes, carrots, water, and salt. Cover and simmer 10 minutes, or until vegetables are tender. Add parsley, sage, paprika, and pepper. Combine 1/2 cup milk and flour in 1 cup measure; blend thoroughly. Add to soup; simmer until slightly thickened, stirring constantly. Add remaining 2 1/2 cups of milk; heat thoroughly. Sprinkle bacon on each serving.

Yield: 6 servings

CAULIFLOWER-POTATO SOUP

3 c. chicken broth
1 head cauliflower (2 lbs.), thinly sliced
4 medium leeks (white part only) or 1 large onion, chopped
1 large potato, washed, peeled, and diced
1 c. half-and-half
1/4 tsp. nutmeg
1/4 tsp. salt
1/8 tsp. white pepper
butter
nutmeg

Combine broth, cauliflower, leeks, and potato in 3-quart saucepan. Bring to a boil; cover and simmer 15 to 20 minutes, or until vegetables are tender.

Place vegetables, 2 cups at a time, in bowl of food processor or blender container; purée. Return to saucepan. Add half-and-half, 1/4 teaspoon nutmeg, salt, and pepper. Heat through; do not boil. Dot each serving with butter and sprinkle with nutmeg.

Yield: 6 servings

POTATO MINESTRONE SOUP

1 meaty beef soup bone
3 Tbsp. salt
1 c. dried red kidney beans
1 lb. beef for stew, cut into bite-size pieces
3 Tbsp. olive oil
2 cloves garlic, minced
1/2 c. parsley, minced
1 medium onion, chopped
1/4 tsp. pepper
3 1/2 c. fresh or canned tomatoes, cut up
2 c. cabbage, finely shredded
1 1/2 c. cut green beans, cut into 1-inch pieces
1 c. celery, diced
1 c. carrots, sliced
2 c. potatoes, washed and diced
2 c. fresh spinach, chopped
1/2 c. elbow macaroni
grated Parmesan cheese

Place soup bone, salt, beans and 5 quarts water in large stockpot. Bring to a boil; skim foam. Cover and simmer 1 1/2 hours. Add stew meat; simmer 2 hours. Heat olive oil in small skillet. Add parsley, and onion; sauté until onion is transparent. Remove soup bone from soup; let cool until easily handled. Remove meat from bone; return meat to soup. Add onion mixture, pepper, tomatoes, cabbage, beans, celery, carrots, and potatoes. Bring to a boil; simmer 15 minutes. Add spinach and macaroni; simmer 20 minutes, or until macaroni is tender. Serve hot, topped with generous amounts of grated Parmesan cheese.

Yield: 10 to 12 servings

GRANNY'S SOUP (Great-Great-Great-Grandma's Soup)

4 potatoes, diced
1 small onion, chopped
4-5 strips bacon
2 slices toast
2 c. creamy milk
dash salt and pepper

Simmer diced potatoes in water until tender. Fry bacon until crisp, sauté onion in bacon drippings. Dice toast and brown in same pan. Crumble bacon. Set aside for topping. Sizzle soup in same pan. Add cream. Heat until hot. Serve with the bacon bits and toast cubes on top.

Yield: 4 servings

Mrs. S.A. Cannady
Roanoke, VA

PUMPKIN-POTATO SOUP

2 Tbsp. margarine
1/4 c. onion, minced
1 tsp. curry powder
1 c. mashed potatoes
3 c. chicken broth
1 can (16 oz.) pumpkin
1 tsp. brown sugar
1/2 tsp. salt
1/8 tsp. pepper
1/8 tsp. mace
1 c. milk
parsley or chives, minced

Melt margarine in 3-quart saucepan. Cook onion until transparent. Remove from heat. Stir in curry powder, potatoes, broth, pumpkin, sugar, salt, pepper, and mace. Return to heat and cook, stirring often, until mixture begins to simmer. Stir in milk. Heat.

Yield: 6 servings

FISH POTATO CHOWDER

2 Tbsp. margarine
1 c. onions, chopped
2 medium potatoes, washed and diced (2 c.)
1/2 c. celery, thinly sliced
2 1/4 c. water
1 tsp. salt
1/2 tsp. dillweed
1/8 tsp. pepper
1 small bay leaf
1 can (13 oz.) evaporated milk, undiluted
1 package (10 oz.) frozen haddock, cod, or similar fish, thawed and
  cut into 1 1/2-inch pieces

Melt margarine in 3-quart saucepan. Cook onions until transparent. Add potatoes, 2 cups water, celery, salt, dillweed, pepper, and bay leaf. Cover and simmer 30 minutes, or until potatoes are tender. Stir in milk. Add fish. Heat to simmering; do not boil. Simmer until fish is opaque and flakes easily. Remove bay leaf.

Yield: 6 servings

VEGETABLE SPLIT PEA SOUP

1 pkg. (1 lb.) split peas
1 can (28 oz.) tomatoes, undrained
1 c. onion, chopped
1 meaty ham bone
1 large potato, washed, peeled, and diced
3 carrots, diced
1 c. celery, sliced
1/4 c. parsley, minced
1/2 tsp. salt
1 bay leaf
croutons

Combine split peas, tomatoes and liquid, onions, ham bone, and 2 quarts water in 6-quart stockpot. Bring to boil; cover and simmer 2 hours. Remove ham bone; let cool until easily handled. Remove meat from bone; return meat to soup. Add potato, carrots, celery, parsley, salt, bay leaf. Simmer 30 minutes, or until vegetables are tender. Discard bay leaf. Serve hot, topped with croutons.

Yield: 8 servings

POTATO-TOMATO BISQUE

1/2 c. butter
1 medium onion, thinly sliced
4 c. ripe tomatoes, peeled and chopped
1 c. tomato juice
3 medium potatoes, washed, peeled, and sliced (3 cups)
1/2 tsp. salt
1/2 tsp. tarragon
1/4 tsp. rosemary
1/8 tsp. white pepper
2 cups half-and-half, heated

Melt butter in 3-quart saucepan. Cook onion until transparent;
do not brown. Add tomatoes and tomato juice; simmer until tomatoes are soft. Add potatoes, salt, tarragon, rosemary, and
pepper. Simmer about 30 minutes, or until potatoes are tender,
stirring occasionally. Remove from heat; cool slightly. Place
mixture, 2 cups at a time, in bowl of food processor or blender
container; purée. Return purée to saucepan; stir in half-and-half.
Sprinkle parsley or chives on each serving.

Yield: 6 to 8 servings

EVERYONE WORKING TOGETHER
TO FIGHT HUNGER

GREAT BEAN AND POTATO SOUP

1 pkg. (1 lb.) great northern beans
1 meaty ham bone or smoked pork hock
1 c. mashed potatoes
2 cloves garlic, minced
1/4 c. parsley, minced

Place beans in large bowl; add water to cover; let stand over-night. Drain beans. Place in 6-quart stockpot. Add ham bone and 3 quarts water. Bring to a boil; cover and simmer 2 hours. Stir in potatoes and garlic. Simmer 1 hour, or until beans are tender. Remove bone from stockpot; let cool until easily handled. Remove meat from bone, dice, and return to soup. Add parsley; heat thoroughly.

Yield: 8 servings

POTATO-TUNA CHOWDER

2 Tbsp. butter
1/2 c. onion, chopped
6 medium potatoes, washed, peeled, and diced
2 medium carrots, diced
1/2 c. celery, diced
1 can (9 1/4 oz.) tuna, undrained
4 c. milk
2 tsp. salt
1/4 tsp. white pepper
1/4 c. parsley, minced

Melt butter in 3 1/2-quart saucepan. Cook onion until trans-parent. Add potatoes, carrots, celery, and 2 cups water; bring to a boil. Cover and simmer 25 to 30 minutes, or until vege-tables are tender, stirring occasionally. Add tuna and milk; heat through. Stir in salt and pepper. Sprinkle parsley on each serving.

Yield: 8 servings

NEW ENGLAND QUAHOG CHOWDER

4 slices bacon, diced
1 large onion, finely chopped
3 cans (6 1/2 oz. each) minced clams
3 medium potatoes, peeled and diced
1 pint half-and-half
1 pint milk
salt and pepper to taste
butter (optional)

Fry diced bacon in a heavy pot until crisp and golden brown. Remove from pan, add the chopped onion to the hot fat, cooking until tender and golden, not brown. Add diced potatoes, juice from drained clams, and just enough water to be seen through the potatoes. Cover the pan and cook the potatoes over medium heat until done. Add clams, half-and-half, milk, and salt and pepper to taste. Heat but do not boil. Two or three tablespoons of butter may be added to the chowder just before serving. The bits of bacon may be added to the chowder, if desired.

Yield: 4-5 servings

GRANDMA DOROTHY'S POTATO SOUP

3 med. potatoes, sliced or cubed
1/4-1/2 c. onion, diced
salt and pepper to taste
2 Tbsp. butter

Cook potatoes in small amount of water, so that you can keep the water from cooking out. When cooked, mash with potato masher. Add 3-4 cups of milk, depending on how much soup you want. Add 2 Tbsp. butter, salt and pepper to taste. Stir and serve hot.

Yield: 4-6 servings

Grandma Dorothy
Frank's recipe
Maureen Franks

CROCK POT SOUP

6 baking potatoes, peeled and grated
2 onions, chopped
1 carrot, pared and grated
3 stalks celery, thinly sliced
4-5 chicken bouillon cubes
1 Tbsp. parsley flakes
5 c. water
1 Tbsp. salt
1/ Tbsp. pepper
1/3 c. butter
`1 13 oz. can evaporated milk

Put all ingredients except milk in a crock pot. Cover and cook on low for 8-10 hours. (High: 3-4 hours) Stir in evaporated milk during the last hour.

Yield: 6-8 servings

Dorothy Schminkey
Arlington, VA

VICHYSSOISE

3 c. potatoes, sliced
3/4 c. leeks, chopped
1/2 c. onion, chopped
1 Tbsp. parsley
1 tsp. salt
1/4 tsp. nutmeg
2 Tbsp. butter
2 c. chicken bouillon
1 c. heavy cream
1 c. milk

Cook all ingredients (except the heavy cream and milk) over medium heat until potatoes are tender. When potatoes are tender, place in blender and blend until smooth. Put in bowl and add cream and milk.

Yield: 6-8 servings

Linda F. Chapman
Manassas, VA

IRISH STEW

3 lbs. neck of lamb
12 medium potatoes
4 large onions, sliced
1 sprig thyme (1 tsp. dried)
2 c. or more water
salt and pepper to taste

Remove the fat from the meat and cut into 8 or 10 sections through the bone. Do not remove the bone, as this adds flavor. Peel the potatoes and slice one-third of them in thin slices. Leave the rest of the potatoes whole.

Into a saucepan, put the thinly sliced potatoes, then a layer of sliced onions, and then the sections of lamb. Season well. Add the thyme and another layer of sliced onion. Cover with the remainder of the potatoes which have been left whole. Season again and add the water. Cover the pot with aluminum foil and then with a very tight-fitting lid.

Bake at 350 degrees for 2 1/2 hours. The stew may also be simmered gently on top of the stove for approximately the same amount of time. The thinly sliced potatoes at the bottom of the pot will dissolve and thicken up the juice.

Yield: 6-8 servings

CREAM OF POTATO SOUP

4 c. potatoes, peeled and cubed
1 c. celery, chopped
1 c. onion, chopped coarsely
2 c. water
2 tsp. salt
1 c. milk
1 c. whipping cream
3 Tbsp. butter or margarine, melted
1 Tbsp. dried parsley flakes
1 tsp. caraway seeds
1/2 tsp. pepper

Combine potatoes, celery, onion, water and salt in large Dutch oven. Simmer covered, about 20 minutes or until potatoes are tender. Mash mixture once or twice with potato masher, leaving some vegetable pieces whole. Stir in remaining ingredients, return to heat and cook, stirring constantly, until soup is thoroughly heated.

Yield: 7 cups

Ruby Shields
Bedford, VA

FINNISH SALMON AND POTATO CHOWDER

1 can pink salmon
3 medium-size potatoes, cubed
1 3/4 c. water
1 medium onion, chopped
4 black peppercorns
1 can skim evaporated milk
1 Tbsp. fresh dill, chopped or 1 tsp. dried dillweed

Add all ingredients to saucepan and cook until potatoes are done.

Yield: 4 servings

Betty Tongue
Lynchburg, VA

RAINY DAY POTATO SOUP

3-4 very large potatoes, diced
2 bunches scallions, chopped (including the tops)
3-4 c. water
4 tsp. salt
white pepper to taste
2 whole bay leaves

Cook above ingredients approximately 45 minutes, till soft. Add 1-2 c. milk if you wish. Enrich with margarine or butter.

Refrigerate all day (or overnight). It thickens when cooled. Use very low temperature to reheat.

Yield: 5-6 servings

Frances Robinson
Santa Fe, NM

EASY CHEESE SOUP

3 cans chicken broth
3 cans cream of potato soup
1 lb. Velveeta cheese
1-2 potatoes
3-4 carrots
3-4 stalks celery
1/2-1 onion

Chop vegetables into bite-size pieces. Boil vegetables separately in water (to cover). Combine broth and soup, add to cooked vegetables. Add Velveeta cheese that has been cubed to soup. Warm thoroughly for cheese to melt.

Yield: 6-8 servings

Laura M. Stephens
Austin, TX

POTATO SOUP

6 potatoes, diced
2 c. water
1 c. celery, sliced
1 c. carrots, scraped & thinly sliced
2 tsp. parsley flakes
2 chicken flavored bouillon cubes
1 tsp. salt
1/3 tsp. pepper
3 c. milk, diluted
1/4 c. all-purpose flour
3/4 lb. processed cheese, cubed

Combine first 8 ingredients and bring to a boil. Cover. Reduce heat. Simmer 7 to 8 minutes or until vegetables are tender. Gradually stir flour into 1/4 c. milk. Stir into soup. Add remaining milk and cheese. Cook until thickened.

Yield: 8 servings

Mary Liz Kehoe
Richmond, VA

ONION-POTATO CHOWDER WITH ITALIAN SAUSAGE

2 large onions
3 Tbsp. butter or margarine
4 c. diced potatoes
4 c. beef broth or bouillon
1 12- to 16-oz. pkg. hot or mild Italian sausages
2 c. milk
1/2 tsp. summer savory or basil
salt and pepper

Finely chop onions to measure 3 cups. Melt butter in Dutch oven, add onions, and cook 2 to 3 minutes. Stir in potatoes and broth. Bring to boil, cover, reduce heat, and simmer 15 minutes. Slice sausages into 1/2-in. thick chunks. Cook in skillet until browned and cooked through. With slotted spoon, add sausages to chowder. Add milk and summer savory or basil. Season to taste with salt and pepper. Heat through.

Yield: 6 servings

SHRIMP POTATO CHOWDER

3 slices bacon
1 c. onion, finely chopped
1 tsp. salt
dash pepper
1 small can shrimp (use small ones or pieces, whatever is cheapest)
2 c. half-and-half
4 Tbsp. butter or margarine

Cook bacon in large pan until crisp, drain off most of the grease, break into pieces. Add onion, cook 5 minutes. Add cubed potatoes, salt, pepper, and 1 cup water. Cook uncovered 15 minutes, till potatoes are tender. Add half-and-half. Rinse shrimp, and add to mixture. Add margarine. Stir and heat, but do not boil.

Yield: 4 large servings

Rachel Scott James
Glasgow, KY

VEGETABLE CHOWDER

1/2 c. rice, uncooked
3 chicken bouillon cubes
5 c. water
1/2 c. diced carrots
1 c. diced potatoes
1 minced onion
1/2 c. finely cut celery
1 c. canned tomatoes
2 tsp. salt
1/8 tsp. pepper
1 c. milk

Combine all of the above except the milk and bring to a boil. Simmer for 45 minutes.

When ready to serve add 1 c. milk. Heat almost to boiling and serve immediately.

Yield: 6 servings

Marian K. Buchanan
Big Island, VA

48

POTATO, CHEESE & CHICKEN SOUP

4 med. potatoes, cubed
1 c. chopped celery
1 c. chopped onions
1 c. diced carrots
1 whole chicken, cut into pieces
1 tsp. marjoram
1 tsp. seasoned salt
4-5 chicken bouillon cubes
2 c. cubed Cheddar cheese

Cover chicken with water and cook until done. Remove chicken from pot and take meat off the bones. Return chicken to pot with 1 qt. of the chicken stock. Add vegetables, spices and bouillon cubes. Simmer until vegetables are done. Add the cheese just before serving.

Yield: 6-8 servings

Laura Conley
Lenexa, KS

TREASURE VALLEY POTATO SOUP

3 Tbsp. butter or margarine
1/4 c. onion, chopped
1/4 c. celery, chopped
3 c. potatoes, diced
1 tsp. marjoram
2 tsp. parsley, minced
1/2 tsp. salt
1 1/2 c. milk
1/2 c. ham, cooked

Melt butter in large saucepan. Sauté onion and celery until tender, about 5 minutes. Add potatoes, marjoram, parsley, salt and enough water to cover potatoes. Bring to a boil and simmer 20 minutes until potatoes are tender. Then add milk and ham stirring occasionally until soup comes to a boil. Serve hot.

Yield: 4 servings

Mary Hancock
Falls Church, VA

SWISS POTATO SOUP

4 small potatoes
1 large flat white turnip
3 c. boiling water
1 qt. scalded milk
4 Tbsp. butter
1/3 c. flour
1 1/2 tsp. salt
1/8 tsp. pepper

Wash, pare, and cut potatoes in halves. Wash, pare, and cut turnips in 1/4-inch slices. Parboil together 10 minutes, drain, add onion and boiling water. Cook until vegetables are soft; drain, reserving water to add to vegetables after rubbing them through sieve. Add milk, reheat, and bind with butter and flour cooked together. Season with salt and pepper.

Yield: 6-8 servings

Ruth Smith Newell

POTATO & DRIED BEEF CHOWDER

3 or 4 medium potatoes, peeled and sliced
1 1/2 c. water, salted
2 Tbsp. butter
1/4 c. onion, chopped
small pkg. dried beef, finely chopped
2 Tbsp. flour
1/3 tsp. pepper
3 c. milk

Cook potatoes in the 1 1/2 c. salted water until just tender. Do not drain. Break up potatoes slightly with a fork in the water they were boiled in. Melt butter in saucepan, add onion, cook until brown, stirring occasionally. Add dried beef; cook, stirring frequently, until edges curl. Add flour and pepper. Blend well. Add milk all at once. Cook, stirring constantly until thickened. Add potatoes and potato water. Reheat.

Yield: 5-6 servings

Gloria Safritt
Lynchburg, VA

Side Dishes

notes

POTATO PUFFS

3/4 c. water
1/4 c. margarine
1 tsp. instant minced onion
1/8 tsp. salt
1/2 c. instant mashed potatoes (dry)
1/4 c. all-purpose flour
2 eggs

Have ready at serving time:
      sour cream
      chopped green onions or snipped chives

Heat water, margarine, onion and salt to rolling boil in 1 1/2-qt. saucepan. Stir in potatoes and flour. Stir vigorously over low heat just until mixture forms a ball, about 1 minute. Remove from heat. Beat in eggs until smooth. Drop dough by heaping tablespoonfuls onto ungreased cookie sheet.

Cook at 400 degrees until puffed and golden, about 30 minutes. (Can be served immediately.) Cool; cover and refrigerate no longer than 2 days.

TO SERVE: About 15 minutes before serving, heat Potato Puffs uncovered on ungreased cookie sheet in a 425 degree oven until hot, about 10 minutes. Serve with sour cream and onions.

Yield: 10 puffs

                          Marian K. Buchanan
                          Big Island, VA

I am only one, but I am still one. I cannot do everything, but still I can do something. And because I cannot do everything, I will not refuse to do the something that I can do.
              -Edward Everett Hale

SWEET POTATO SOUFFLÉ

4 c. sweet potatoes, mashed
1 stick margarine or butter
pinch of salt
2 tsp. vanilla
1/2 c. milk
4 eggs
2 c. sugar

Combine the above ingredients and place in a large casserole dish.

Topping:
2 cans (small cans) crushed pineapple
1/2 c. flour
1 c. sugar
2 eggs, well beaten
1 stick melted margarine

Combine the above for the topping and pour over potato mixture. Bake 30 minutes in a 350 degree oven.

Yield: 6-8 servings

F. Beadles
Richmond, VA

MARGARET'S SWEET POTATO CASSEROLE

1 large can sweet potatoes, drained
1 c. sugar
2 eggs
3/4 stick butter, melted
pinch salt
1 tsp. orange extract
dash of cinnamon
1/2 c. liquid from potatoes

Mash potatoes, add all ingredients. Bake 15 minutes at 400 degrees. Take out and top with miniature marshmallows. Top with the following.

54

Topping:

1 c. corn flakes, crushed
3/4 c. butter, melted
3/4 c. brown sugar
1/2 c. pecans, finely chopped

Mix well. Spread on sweet potatoes and return to oven for 15 minutes. Do not over cook.

Yield: 6-8 servings

Trudy Thaxton
Bedford, VA

SWEET POTATO CARAMEL

1/2 c. evaporated milk
1 egg
3 c. sweet potatoes, cooked and mashed
3 Tbsp. butter
1 8 oz. pkg. dates, sliced

Add milk and egg to mashed potatoes. Beat well until smooth. Melt butter. Add dates and sauté for two minutes, stirring constantly. Add potatoes to mixture and blend until dates are blended in. Put in large casserole dish.

Topping:

1/2 c. maple syrup
3 Tbsp. butter

Heat syrup and butter until melted. Pour over top of casserole. Bake at 350 degrees for 40 minutes. If desired, serve topped with a dollop of sour cream and garnish with whole dates.

Yield: 8 generous servings

Mrs. Roland Holmes
Pittsburg, KS

GERMAN FRIED POTATOES

Wash, pare and slice potatoes thin, using vegetable slicer. Let stand 1/2 hr. in cold water; drain and dry between towels. Heat fat in heavy frying pan, lay in potatoes, sprinkle with salt, cover pan and cook slowly until tender and brown. If desired, cook finely chopped onion with potatoes. Stir and turn occasionally.

Yield: Use one potato per serving

Ruth Smith Newell

CURRIED POTATOES

1/4 c. butter
1 small onion, finely chopped
3 c. cold, boiled potatoes, cubed
1/2 - 3/4 c. chicken broth
1/2 Tbsp. curry powder
1/2 Tbsp. lemon juice
salt & pepper

Cook onion in butter until yellow. Add potatoes and cook until butter is absorbed. Add stock and seasonings. Cook until potatoes have absorbed broth.

Yield: 6 servings

Ruth Smith Newell

"What small potatoes we all are, compared with what we might be!"
-Charles Dudley Warner

CRANBERRY SWEET POTATOES

5 sweet potatoes or 1 large can of sweet potatoes
rind from 1 orange
1/2 c. orange juice
1/4 c. brown sugar
dash of salt
1 can whole cranberry sauce

Cut potatoes in large chunks and place in a greased casserole dish. Mix together the orange rind, orange juice, brown sugar and salt. Pour mixture over the potatoes. Spread the can of cranberries over the top and bake at 350 degrees for 35-45 minutes.

Yield: 6 servings

Dorothy Schminkey
Arlington, VA

SCALLOPED POTATOES WITH CUCUMBERS

1/2 lb. sharp cheese, shredded
4 c. sliced potatoes
1 cucumber, sliced
2 Tbsp. flour
1 tsp. salt
1/8 tsp. pepper
2 Tbsp. butter
2 c. milk

Grease a baking dish. Arrange potatoes, cheese, and cucumbers in layers. Sprinkle each layer with flour, salt and pepper. Melt butter and pour over each layer. Heat milk and pour over top. Bake covered for 30 minutes and then uncovered for 20 minutes at 375 degrees.

Yield: 6 servings

Dorothy Schminkey
Arlington, VA

HAWAIIAN SWEET POTATOES

1 c. sugar
2 cans sweet potatoes
1 stick butter
2 Tbsp. cornstarch
1 small can pineapple rings
1/4 c. coconut
1/2 c. whipping cream
1 tsp. butternut flavoring
1/4 tsp. pumpkin pie spice mix
6 cherries

Pour off all syrup of pineapple and potatoes into saucepan. Add sugar, cornstarch, and butter. Cook until it thickens. Remove from heat and add spice, flavoring, and stir well. Whip cream and fold in. Pour over sweet potatoes and place pineapple rings on potatoes. Sprinkle on coconut and add cherries. Bake at 350 degrees about 20 minutes.

Yield: 6-8 servings

Ann Goff
Big Island, VA

SHREDDED SWEET POTATOES

2 c. sweet potatoes, shredded
1 c. crushed pineapple
3 eggs
2 Tbsp. flour
1 1/2 c. sugar
4 Tbsp. butter
1 c. milk

Cream butter and eggs and beat. Add flour and mix thoroughly. Add the pineapple, then milk and sweet potatoes. Pour into buttered baking dish and bake at 350 degrees for 50 minutes or until brown and mixture is firm.

Yield: 6 servings

Ann Goff
Big Island, VA

58

HERBED POTATO BAKE

1/4 c. margarine, melted
1 (1 3/8 oz.) envelope onion soup mix
1 Tbsp. rosemary
3 baking potatoes, unpeeled

Combine margarine, soup mix, and rosemary. Set aside. Scrub potatoes and slice 1/2 inch thick. Combine margarine mixture with potatoes and toss gently. Arrange in shallow covered baking dish. Bake at 350 degrees for 1 hour.

Yield: 3-4 servings

CARROT-POTATO PUDDING

2 carrots, peeled and sliced
2 potatoes, peeled and cubed
1 egg
2 Tbsp. sour cream (optional)
2 Tbsp. onion, finely minced
1/2 tsp. salt
1/4 tsp. pepper
2 oz. (1/2 c.) Cheddar cheese
1 Tbsp. margarine

Cook carrots in water for 10 minutes. Add potatoes and cook 15 minutes more. Drain carrots and potatoes and mash. Add egg, sour cream, onion, salt and pepper, mixing well. Beat in grated cheese. Spoon into 1 1/2-quart casserole dish. Bake at 350 degrees for 30 minutes. Dot top with margarine. Place under broiler for 3 minutes. Garnish with orange slice if desired.

Yield: 6-8 servings

Kathryn L. Kesler
Roanoke, VA

SCALLOPED CHEESE AND POTATOES

4 c. potatoes, thinly sliced
3/4 c. onion, finely chopped
3/4 tsp. salt
1 can Cheddar cheese soup
1/2 c. milk
1 Tbsp. Worcestershire sauce

In a well buttered 2-quart casserole dish, arrange in alternate layers potatoes, onions, and salt. Repeat 3 times. In a small saucepan heat soup with milk and Worcestershire sauce. Pour over potato mixture. Cover and bake in a preheated oven of 375 degrees for 45 minutes. Remove cover and bake 15 minutes longer. May take up to 1 1/2 hours to fully cook.

Yield: 4-6 servings

Susan Layne
Bedford, VA

HASH BROWN CASSEROLE

2 lb. pkg. hash browns or equal amount of raw potatoes
2 cans cream of potato soup
1 medium onion, chopped
1 c. sour cream
1 c. sharp cheese
salt and pepper to taste

Mix all ingredients. Bake at 300 degrees for 1 1/2 hours.

Yield: 6-8 servings

Leta Lester
Forest, VA

POTATO FILLING CASSEROLE

4 c. mashed potatoes, seasoned with butter, salt and pepper
3 eggs
1 large onion, chopped and browned in butter
1 c. cubed bread, crusts or stale bread may be used
1 Tbsp. dried parsley flakes

Mix all ingredients together and put into a greased casserole.
Dot with butter. Bake at 350 degrees for about one hour or
until top is nicely browned.

Note: This recipe does not need to be exact. You can use leftover mashed potatoes, you can increase the eggs, onions, bread,
and parsley. It can also be made the day before you plan to
serve it. Goes especially well with fowl, but also good with pork
or beef with lots of good gravy.

Yield: 6 servings

Dorothy Schminkey
Arlington, VA

GERRY'S OVEN-CANDIED SWEET POTATOES

8 medium-size sweet potatoes
1 c. brown sugar, firmly packed
1 tsp. light corn syrup
1/2 c. orange juice
1/4 c. butter
1 c. white sugar
1 tsp. orange rind, grated

Heat oven to 450 degrees. Peel potatoes and cut in half lengthwise. Place in an ungreased 2-quart casserole. Add the com-
bined other ingredients. Bake covered for 30 minutes. Uncover
and bake 20 minutes longer, basting as needed. Check to see
when tender and golden color and that the sauce has thickened
to your wishes.

Yield: 10 servings

Trudy Thaxton
Bedford, VA

GOLDEN PARMESAN POTATOES

4 very large potatoes
1/4 c. flour
1/4 c. Parmesan cheese
3/4 tsp. salt
1/8 tsp. pepper
1/3 c. butter

Combine flour, Parmesan cheese, salt, and pepper in a bag.
Pare potatoes and cut in 6 pieces each. Shake potatoes in bag
and coat with dry mixture. Melt butter in 9 X 13 baking pan.
Place potatoes in pan and bake at 375 degrees for 1 hour turning once, or until nicely browned and cooked.

Yield: 4-6 servings

Anne Lillie
Alexandria, VA

APRICOT SWEET POTATOES

1 1 lb. 1 oz. can vacuum packed sweet potato slices
1 1/4 c. brown sugar
1 tsp. orange peel, grated
1/2 tsp. cinnamon, ground
2 Tbsp. butter
1 1/2 Tbsp. cornstarch
1 1lb. 1 oz. can apricot halves
1/2 c. pecan halves
1/4 tsp. salt

Put potatoes in greased 10 x 6 baking dish. Combine brown
sugar, cornstarch, orange peel, salt, and cinnamon. Drain
apricots, reserving 1 cup syrup, add syrup to sugar mixture.
Simmer 3 minutes. Add apricots, butter, and pecans. Boil for
2 minutes. Pour over potatoes. Bake uncovered 25 minutes at
375 degrees.

Yield: 6 servings

Mrs. R. E. Perrow
Lynchburg, VA

COUNTRY STYLE SCALLOPED POTATOES

3 large potatoes
3 medium onions
1 stick margarine
1/2 c. milk
1 c. cheddar cheese
salt to taste

In greased baking dish, place a layer of potatoes, onion, cheese, and butter. Repeat until all are used. Pour milk and salt over potatoes; cover and cook in oven at 400 degrees until done.

Yield: 4-6 servings

Ann Goff
Big Island, VA

SOUR CREAM POTATOES

1 can cream of chicken soup (undiluted)
1/2 stick margarine
1 c. sharp cheese, grated
1 c. sour cream
1 small bunch green onion tops, chopped
2 12 oz. pkgs. frozen shredded hash browns

Place unthawed potatoes in 8 x 12-inch pan. Heat soup, margarine, cheese and sour cream over medium heat until cheese is melted. Add chopped green onion tops to mixture. Spoon mixture over potatoes. Cook at 325 degrees for 30-45 minutes.

Yield: 6-8 servings

Marolyn Carter
Roanoke, VA

FLEMISH POTATOES

2 slices bacon, cut into pieces
1 small onion, minced
2 potatoes, diced
dash of pepper
1/4 tsp. salt
1/4 tsp. mixed herbs
1/4 tsp. bay leaf, crushed
3/4 c. water

Sauté bacon in skillet, remove bacon from skillet. In same skillet, sauté onion. Add diced potatoes, herbs, spices, bacon and water. Cover and cook over low heat until potatoes are done. Do not drain.

Yield: 2-3 servings

Martha Cragen
Charlottesville, VA

POTATO MUSHROOM PATTIES

1 medium onion, peeled and minced
2 Tbsp. butter
1 c. mushrooms, chopped
2 c. mashed potatoes
1 egg
salt to taste
pepper to taste
fine dry bread crumbs
butter or oil for frying

Sauté onion in butter in skillet until tender. Add mushrooms and sauté for 3 minutes. Mix with potatoes, egg, salt and pepper. Shape into flat, round or oval patties and roll in bread crumbs. Fry in butter or oil until golden on all sides.

Yield: 3-4 servings

Alice Gunderson
Alexandria, VA

GRAVY STYLE POTATOES

4 Tbsp. butter
1 medium onion, sliced
6 medium potatoes, sliced 1/4 inch thick
1 tsp. salt
1/4 tsp. black pepper
water not quite covering

Melt butter in large fry pan and brown potatoes and onions, stirring often. Add salt, pepper, and water. Stir. Cover and simmer until tender, about 20 minutes. Uncover and let gravy cook down to the thickness that you like. You may make this as large a quantity as you wish.

Yield: 4-6 servings

Frances Wakefield
Woodbridge, VA

TASTY POTATOES

1 large potato, washed and sliced (don't peel)
1 large onion, sliced
butter as desired
salt and pepper to taste

Place potato on a sheet of aluminum foil. Top with onion. Then add butter, salt, and pepper. Wrap up the foil and bake for 1 hour at 350 degrees. This also works great on the grill.

Yield: 1 serving

A. Pawlowski
Manassas, VA

EASY CHEESE POTATOES

1 (2-lb.) pkg. frozen hash brown potatoes, partially thawed
1 (16-oz.) container sour cream
2 c. shredded Colby cheese
1 c. shredded Monterey Jack cheese
1/2 c. chopped onion
1/2 c. chopped green pepper
1 (2-oz.) jar sliced pimentos, drained
1 Tbsp. chicken-flavor instant bouillon

Preheat oven to 350 degrees. In large bowl, combine all ingredients except 1/2 c. of the Colby cheese; mix well. Turn into buttered 13 X 9-inch baking dish. Bake 55 to 60 minutes or until potatoes are tender. Top with remaining cheese; bake 3 to 5 minutes or until cheese melts. Let stand 5 minutes. Serve.

Yield: 6-8 servings.

SCALLOPED POTATOES WITH HERBS

4 c. thinly sliced potatoes
salt & paprika to taste
1/2 tsp. dried marjoram
1/2 tsp. savory
1 tsp chopped parsley
1/2 tsp. chopped chives
1/2 tsp. thyme
3 Tbsp. butter
1 c. milk
1 c. water
1 c. soft bread crumbs, buttered

Place half the potatoes in a greased baking dish and sprinkle with salt and paprika. Add half the herbs and dot with half the butter. Repeat layers. Pour milk and water over potatoes and cover. Bake at 375 degrees for 40 minutes. Remove cover and sprinkle with bread crumbs. Bake for 15 minutes longer or until brown.

Yield: 6 servings.

CHEESY NEW POTATOES

12 medium new potatoes
salt and pepper to taste
16 slices bacon
1/2 c. melted butter
2 c. Old English cheese, grated
1/4 c. parsley to garnish, chopped

Wash and cube unpeeled potatoes, and boil until just tender. Remove from heat, drain and season to taste with salt and pepper. Place layer of potatoes in two-quart casserole, half the bacon, half the butter and half the cheese. Repeat layers. Heat 20-30 minutes in 350 degree oven or until cheese is bubbly. Remove from oven and garnish with parsley. Freezes well.

Yield: 6-8 servings

Margaret Gaddy
Alexandria, VA

NEW POTATOES WITH PARSLEY BUTTER

1 3/4 lbs. new potatoes, washed and scrubbed
1/4 c. butter or margarine, melted
1/3 c. fresh parsley, chopped
salt and pepper to taste

Pare a 1-inch strip around center of each potato, if desired. Cover potatoes with water; cook, covered, over medium heat 25 minutes or until tender, drain and set aside.

Combine remaining ingredients stirring well. Pour over potatoes coating thoroughly.

Yield: 4-6 servings

Charlotte Meredith
Cullman, AL

SWEET-SOUR YAMS AND PINEAPPLE

1 20-oz. can sliced pineapple
1 Tbsp. cornstarch
1/4 tsp. salt
3 Tbsp. vinegar
2 16-oz. cans yams, drained
4 green onions, diagonally sliced
1/2 c. diagonally sliced celery
1/2 c. green pepper chunks
1 Tbsp. oil

Drain the pineapple and reserve syrup. Combine reserved
syrup with cornstarch and salt in a saucepan and cook, stirring, until sauce boils and thickens. Stir in the vinegar. Add
the yams and pineapple slices and pour into a casserole. Cover.
Bake at 350 degrees for about 25 minutes. Cook the onion,
celery and green pepper in oil in a saucepan for about 4 minutes. Stir into yam mixture and serve at once.

Yield: 8 servings

POTATOES ANNA

6 medium potatoes (about 2 lbs.)
1/2 c. margarine, melted
1 tsp. salt
1/2 tsp. pepper

Peel potatoes and slice thinly. Immediately toss slices in melted
margarine, salt and pepper to coat thoroughly, and to prevent
browning. Arrange slices in layers or overlapping circles in generously buttered 1 1/2-qt. baking dish. Bake at 425 degrees for
30-40 minutes or until potatoes are tender. Invert onto serving
platter. Serve hot; cut into squares or wedges.

Yield: 6-8 servings

Mary Hille McCoy
Monterey, VA

ESCALLOPED POTATOES

4 medium potatoes, raw, peeled and sliced 1/4 inch thick
1 medium onion, sliced
4 oz. butter (one stick)
3/4 tsp. salt
1/4 tsp. pepper
2 c. milk

Butter casserole. Add 1 layer potatoes. Dot with butter, salt, and pepper. Add layer of onion slices. Add layer of potato slices and repeat layers until casserole is 3/4 full. Dot top with butter, salt, and pepper. Pour scalded milk over potatoes until it reaches the top layer. Bake in 350 degree oven for 1 hour or until potatoes are soft.

Yield: 5 servings

Florence Bessie Layton
Alexandria, VA

LEMON POTATO WEDGES

vegetable spray
1 Tbsp. margarine, melted
3/4 tsp. lemon rind, grated
1 Tbsp. lemon juice
3/4 tsp. dillweed
3 medium unpeeled baking potatoes (1-1 1/2 lb.)
2 Tbsp. grated Parmesan cheese

Line baking sheet with aluminum foil and coat with cooking spray. Combine margarine and next 3 ingredients in small bowl. Cut each potato (unpeeled) into 4 wedges. Brush cut edges with margarine mixture. Dredge in cheese. Place on baking sheet. Bake at 425 degrees for 25-30 minutes or until potatoes are tender.

Yield: 6 servings

J. R. Wyatt
Lynchburg, VA

PAN-BROILED GRATED POTATOES

3 medium-size baking potatoes, washed and grated, skin and all
2 Tbsp. grated onion
2 Tbsp. butter
2 Tbsp. vegetable oil

Melt butter and oil in skillet to the point of fragrance. Spread
the potatoes in the skillet to a depth of about 1/4 inch. Cook
covered over medium low heat until bottom is browned. Reverse
and brown on the other side. Season to taste.

Yield: 4 servings

Mae Kelly
Lakeland, FL

FRESH POTATO MELANGE

2-4 Tbsp. butter
3 1/2 c. potatoes, pared and cut in strips
1 c. onion, chopped
3/4 c. carrot, thinly sliced
1 c. celery, sliced
1 clove garlic, chopped
2 c. chicken broth
1 bay leaf
1/4 tsp. dried leaf thyme, crumbled
1/4 tsp. salt
1/8 tsp. pepper

Melt butter in large skillet. Sauté potatoes, onion, carrot,
celery, and garlic 2 to 3 minutes, stirring occasionally. Stir in
broth, bay leaf, thyme, salt, and pepper. Bring to boiling,
cover, reduce heat, and simmer 10 minutes. Uncover; cook 5
minutes longer. With slotted spoon remove vegetables to serving bowl. Reduce cooking liquid over high heat until slightly
thickened. Pour over vegetables.

Yield: 4-6 servings

POTATOES MONTROUGE

4 potatoes
4 carrots
1 egg
3 Tbsp. grated Parmesan cheese
2 Tbsp. butter
2 Tbsp. sour cream
salt and pepper
dash of dry mustard

Peel and cut up potatoes and carrots in chunks and put in boiling salted water. Cook until soft. Drain and mash. Beat in rest of ingredients. Arrange in oven-proof serving dish and sprinkle with some cheese and dots of butter. Brown under the broiler quickly.

Yield: 4-6 servings

SWEET POTATO AND APPLE SCALLOP I

2 c. cooked sweet potatoes, sliced
2 c. thinly sliced cooking apples
3/4 c. fine dry bread crumbs
1 c. maple syrup
1/4 c. butter
chopped walnuts

Arrange sweet potatoes, apples and crumbs in alternate layers in buttered baking dish. Add syrup, dot with butter, sprinkle with nuts and bake, covered, at 425 degrees until apples are tender.

Yield: 4-6 servings

SOUTHWESTERN POTATOES WITH A TRIO OF SAUCES

2 1/4 lbs. medium russet or red potatoes, unpeeled
3 Tbsp. safflower oil
1 1/2 tsp. ground cumin
1 tsp. salt

sour cream
processor Guacamole*
Salsa Cruda**

Position rack in center of oven and then preheat at 450 degrees.

Use Thick Slicer: Stand potatoes in feed tube of food processor and slice using firm pressure or slice by hand in 1/2-inch slices.

Transfer potatoes to large bowl. Add oil, cumin and salt and toss to coat thoroughly. Spread potatoes in single layer on baking sheet. Bake 17 minutes. Turn with spatula. Cook until crisp and golden, about 11 minutes.

Arrange 6 potato slices in circle on each plate, overlapping slightly. Top 2 with sour cream, 2 with guacamole and 2 with salsa. Serve sour cream, guacamole and salsa separately on the side.

Yield: 6 servings

*Processor Guacamole

3 Tbsp. loosely packed fresh cilantro leaves
1 jalapeno chili, seeded
1 small onion, quartered
3 large very ripe avocados, pitted and peeled
1 1/2 tsp. fresh lime juice
1/4 tsp. salt

Use Steel Knife: Place cilantro in work bowl. With machine running, drop chili and onion through feed tube and mince. Stop machine. Add avocados, lime juice and salt and chop coarsely using 7 to 8 on/off turns. Do not over process. May be prepared 2 hours ahead. Transfer to bowl; press piece of plastic directly onto surface. Chill; stir before using.

Yield: 2 1/2 cups

**Salsa Cruda

1/2 c. loosely packed fresh cilantro leaves
1 large garlic clove
1 jalapeno or serrano chili, seeded if desired
1/2 small onion, halved
2 medium tomatoes, quartered and seeded
1 tsp. red wine vinegar
1 tsp. light olive oil
1/4 tsp. salt

Use Steel Knife: Place cilantro in work bowl. With machine running, drop garlic and chili through feed tube and mince. Add onion and process until minced. Stop machine. Add tomatoes, vinegar, oil and salt and chop coarsely using about 10 on/off turns; do not over process. May be prepared 4 hours ahead Cover tightly and refrigerate. Drain any excess liquid. Adjust seasoning to taste.

Yield: 2 cups

LEMON POTATOES
MICROWAVE RECIPE

3 medium potatoes, Idaho type (do not peel)
3 Tbsp. butter or margarine
2 Tbsp. fresh lemon juice
1/2 tsp. paprika
3 Tbsp. grated Parmesan cheese
grated lemon peel

Cut potatoes into quarters lengthwise. Melt butter in long pyrex dish with lemon juice. Roll potatoes in lemon butter. Leave in dish with peel side up. Cook uncovered approximately 12 minutes. Turn potatoes halfway through. Mix the parmesan cheese, paprika and some grated lemon peel. Sprinkle over potatoes for the last few minutes of cooking time. Potatoes cooking time: 7 minutes per pound at 100% power. (Cooking time may vary according to your microwave's wattage.)

Yield: 4 servings

Mrs. Robert S. Estes
Marietta, GA

POTATO DUMPLINGS

6 medium-size baking potatoes
2 eggs
1 1/2 tsp. salt
1/2 c. flour
croutons, optional
1/2 c. butter
1/4 c. dry bread crumbs

Boil the potatoes in their jackets until tender, peel and rice them. Add the eggs, salt, and flour. Beat the batter with a fork until fluffy. Roll it lightly into balls around a crouton, about an inch in diameter. Drop the balls into gently boiling salted water and cook about 10 minutes. Drain them well. If you did not put a crouton in the middle, melt 1/2 c. butter, stir in 1/4 cup dry bread crumbs, and pour over dumplings.

Yield: 8-10 servings

Mae Kelly
Lakeland, FL

74

BOXTY PANCAKES
Irish Potato Pancakes

3 medium-sized potatoes (about 1 lb.), preferably baking pota-
    toes
1/4 c. milk
1/2 tsp. caraway seeds (optional)
1/2 c. flour
3 to 4 Tbsp. butter or rendered bacon fat
1/2 tsp. salt
crisp fried bacon (optional)

Peel the potatoes and drop them into a bowl of cold water to
prevent their discoloring. In a large bowl, stir together the
flour, salt and milk, and optional caraway seeds. One at a
time, pat the potatoes dry and grate them coarsely into a sieve
or colander. As you proceed, press each potato firmly down
into the sieve with the back of a large spoon to remove its
moisture, then immediately stir the gratings into the flour and
milk mixture.

In a heavy 8 to 10-inch skillet, melt 2 Tbsp. of the butter or fat
over moderate heat. When the foam begins to subside, pour in
about 1 Tbsp. of batter for each pancake. Cook 3 or 4 pancakes at a time, leaving enough space between them so that
they can spread into 4-inch cakes. Fry them for about 3 minutes on each side, or until they are golden brown and crisp
around the edges. Transfer the finished pancakes to a heated
plate and drape foil over them to keep them warm while you
cook the remaining cakes, adding fat to the pan when necessary. Serve the pancakes as soon as they are all cooked,
accompanied, if you wish, by crisp bacon.

Yield: 10 pancakes

GARDEN-TOPPED POTATOES

4 large potatoes
1/2 c. margarine
2 medium onions, chopped
1 green pepper, cut into strips
1 garlic clove, minced
2 fresh tomatoes, peeled, cut in wedges
1 small zucchini, sliced
1/3 c. grated Parmesan cheese
1/4 tsp. salt
pinch black pepper
8 oz. plain yogurt

Wash and prick potatoes. Bake at 450 degrees about 40-50 minutes. Turn oven off and prepare the vegetable topping. In a large skillet melt the margarine. Cook onion, green pepper and garlic until vegetables are crisp-tender, about 3 minutes. Stir in tomatoes and zucchini. Cook, stirring often, 2 minutes longer. Stir in Parmesan cheese, salt and pepper and yogurt. Continue cooking, stirring constantly, about 1 minute longer. Split tops of baked potatoes, and fluff with fork; spoon vegetable mixture over them.

Yield: 4 servings

SOUR CREAM POTATO CASSEROLE

1 c. dairy sour cream
1 c. large curd cottage cheese
2 c. mashed potatoes
1 small onion, minced
1 (4 oz. jar) pimento, drained and chopped
2 eggs
2 Tbsp. soft butter
3/4 tsp. salt

Combine all ingredients and blend. Spread in buttered 1 1/2-quart baking dish. Bake in 350 degree oven for 1 hour.

Yield: 6 servings

Mrs. Robert S. Estes
Marietta, GA

EASY SWEET ONIONS AND POTATOES

4 med. Idaho potatoes, peeled & sliced
3 large sweet onions (or 5 yellow onions) peeled and sliced
Velveeta or other mild cheese
1 c. ranch-style dressing

In saucepan with water to cover, boil potatoes until just tender.
Drain. Place alternate layers of potatoes and onions in 10 X 13-inch glass dish. Slice cheese, arrange slices on top of potato
and onion mixture. Top with ranch dressing. Cover and micro-wave on high for 4-5 minutes. For a conventional oven, cover
and bake at 350 degrees for 20 minutes.

Yield: 4-6 servings

Diane Schorn
Deerfield, IL

PARSLEY POTATOES AND CARROTS

4 new red potatoes, about 3/4 lb.
12 baby carrots, about 1/2 lb.
salt to taste, if desired
freshly ground pepper to taste
1 Tbsp. butter
1 Tbsp. parsley, finely chopped

Cut the unpeeled potatoes into quarters and put in a saucepan.
Trim and scrape the carrots and add them to the saucepan.
Add water to cover and salt to taste. Bring to boil and cook
until the vegetables are tender, about 8 minutes. Drain and add
the pepper and the butter. Stir to coat the vegetables. Serve
sprinkled with chopped parsley.

Yield: 4 servings

NONA'S GNOCCHI (ITALIAN POTATO DUMPLINGS)

2 lbs. white potatoes (dry mealy ones work best)
1 egg
1 lb. flour
3 qts. rapidly boiling water with 2 Tbsp. salt
tomato sauce
grated Parmesan cheese

Scrub potatoes but do not peel. Place in saucepan and cover with water. Cover and cook over med. heat until tender when pierced with a fork. Drain and cover snugly with towel to absorb some moisture. After 5 minutes put potatoes through a ricer or mash with a fork. While potatoes are still warm, stir in egg. Using your hands, gradually mix in enough flour to make a medium soft dough. Turn onto floured board. Knead about 5 times or until ingredients are blended. If dough is sticky, flour hands to knead.

Make a test gnocchi (dumpling) and drop in boiling salted water. If it falls apart, add more flour to dough. Pinch off a piece of dough about the size of an apricot. Roll under palm of hand until 1/2 inch thick (the way children make snakes with playdough). Cut into 3/4-inch lengths. Toss lightly in flour. Press tightly with tines of fork dipped in flour. Arrange in single layer on cookie sheet or waxed paper. May be frozen at this point. To serve, drop 20 gnocchi at a time in boiling, salted water. When they float (about 3 minutes) remove with slotted spoon to serving dish. Keep warm, when all are cooked, cover with sauce and sprinkle with Parmesan cheese.

Yield: 6 servings

Patsy Martin
Big Island, VA

78

PAPRIKA POTATOES

2 1/2 c. partially cooked potatoes, sliced in round slices
2 Tbsp. bacon fat
3/4 c. onion, chopped
1 tsp. paprika
1 tsp. salt
1/3 tsp. pepper
1 1/4 c. sour cream
1 Tbsp. parsley

Heat bacon fat in skillet, add onion, paprika, salt & pepper.
Remove from heat and blend in sour cream. Add potatoes, mix
gently and thoroughly. Cover skillet and cook over very low heat
about 30 minutes. Occasionally turn potatoes in sauce. Garnish
with chopped parsley.

Yield: 3-4 servings

Marion Proehl
Lynchburg, VA

MEXICAN POTATO BALLS

1 1/2 c. hot mashed potatoes
2 eggs, beaten
1/4 tsp. chili powder
1/2 tsp. salt
1/8 tsp. dry mustard
1 tsp. grated onion
1 tsp. milk
1/2 c. dry bread crumbs
1/2 c. shredded cheese

Combine potatoes, eggs, seasonings, and milk. Blend cheese
and bread crumbs. Add one-half to the potato mixture.
Shape into balls and roll in remaining cheese and bread
crumbs. Fry in deep fat until golden brown. Drain.

Yield: 4 servings

Mary Hille McCoy
Monterey, VA

COLCANNON

1 lb. potatoes, unpeeled
1 lb. green cabbage, shredded, approximately 4 cups
1 large onion, chopped (1 c.)
1/4 c. skim or low fat milk
1 Tbsp. butter or margarine
3 oz. sharp Cheddar, grated
freshly ground black pepper to taste
salt to taste

Boil potatoes in lightly salted water until very tender, but not mush. Drain, reserving cooking liquid, and set aside to cool. Using potato water, boil cabbage and onion about 5 minutes. Drain and set aside. When potatoes are cool enough, peel off skin, place in bowl with milk and butter or margarine, mash until smooth. Add cabbage and onion. Mix 2/3 of cheese with potato mixture. Season with pepper and salt. Transfer to greased casserole or shallow baking dish. Sprinkle remaining cheese on top. Heat through in 350 degree oven or in microwave till cheese melts.

Yield: 4-6 servings.

Judy Robertson
Lynchburg, VA

GOLDEN POTATOES

5 medium potatoes
3-4 carrots
butter
salt
pepper

Cook potatoes and carrots together. Cream as for mashed potatoes. Add butter, salt, and pepper to taste.

Yield: 4 servings

Fanchon Miller
Lynchburg, VA

POTATO OMELETTE

4 medium white potatoes, cooked, peeled and sliced
1 medium white onion, peeled and diced
2 Tbsp. fresh parsley, diced
2 Tbsp. margarine
4 eggs
2 Tbsp. grated Parmesan cheese

Sauté onions in margarine until they are translucent. Add sliced potatoes and brown one side. Turn potatoes and arrange potatoes one layer thick. Beat together 4 eggs, 2 Tbsp. water, and parsley. Pour mixture over potatoes and sprinkle Parmesan cheese over top. Cover frying pan and allow egg mixture to cook. Cut into four servings.

Yield: 4 servings

Linda Youngstrom
Media, PA

CRUNCH-TOP POTATOES

1/3 c. butter or margarine
3 or 4 large baking potatoes, pared, and cut into 1/2-inch slices
3/4 c. crushed corn flakes
1 1/2 c. sharp cheese, shredded
2 tsp. salt
1 1/2 tsp. paprika

Melt butter in jelly-roll pan in 375 degree oven. Add single layer of potatoes, turn once in butter. Mix remaining ingredients; sprinkle over potatoes. Bake 1/2 hour or till done.

Yield: 4-6 servings

Mrs. Roland Holmes
Pittsburg, KS

SWEET POTATOES TZIMMES

2 cans (16 oz. each) sweet potatoes in heavy syrup, drained, or
    enough fresh sweet potatoes, baked and skinned, to make 2
    cups when sliced
1 can (20 oz.) unsweetened apple slices, drained
1/2 c. dark seedless raisins
1/4 c. coarsely chopped English walnuts
1/2 c. honey
1/4 c. margarine
1 tsp. grated orange peel
1/2 tsp. salt
1/3 tsp. ground cinnamon
1/3 tsp. ground ginger

Cut sweet potatoes into 1/4-inch slices. Layer in a lightly
greased 1 1/2-quart casserole with apple slices, raisins, and
walnuts. Combine honey, margarine, orange peel, salt, cinnamon, and ginger in a saucepan. Heat until margarine is melted
and mixture is well blended. Pour over layered mixture. Bake
uncovered at 350 degrees about one hour, basting occasionally.

Yield: 6-8 servings

Lois Kessler
Livermore, CA

O'BRIEN POTATOES

4 medium potatoes, peeled and diced
1/4 c. shortening
1 onion, finely chopped
1 small jar pimentos, chopped
parsley, minced

Sauté potatoes in the shortening in a heavy skillet, turning
more or less constantly, until brown and tender. Add the onion
as potatoes begin to brown. When potatoes are almost cooked,
gently stir in pimentos. When hot, turn out on a serving dish
and sprinkle with minced parsley.

Yield: 4 servings

Ray A. Buchanan
Big Island, VA

POTATO PANCAKES

4 c. grated potatoes (about 3 large white skinned potatoes, not
   baking potatoes)
3 Tbsp. cream
1 egg, beaten
1/2 tsp. salt
1/4 c. flour
oil

Wash potatoes, peel and grate. Put in a straining cloth. Mash
out some of the juice. Add cream, egg, salt, and flour. Mix well.
Fry in 1/2-inch oil, 5-8 minutes, until golden on both sides.

Yield: 6 servings

Hilda Reeh
Needville, TX

POTATOES SAVOYARD

2 lbs. potatoes, peeled & thinly sliced
6 Tbsp. butter
2 Tbsp. snipped parsley
1 c. Cheddar cheese, grated
1 tsp. salt
1/8 tsp. pepper
1 can beef broth

Preheat oven to 425 degrees. Grease 2-qt. shallow baking dish
with 2 Tbsp. butter. Layer half of potatoes in baking dish.
Dot with 2 Tbsp. butter. Mix parsley, salt, pepper, and cheese
using half of mixture on first layer of potatoes. Add second
layer of potatoes, cover with remainder of cheese mixture. Dot
with the last 2 Tbsp. butter. Heat beef broth to boiling and
pour over the casserole. Bake about 1 hour or until potatoes
are tender.

Yield: 6-8 servings

Mrs. James Yates
Lynchburg, VA

SWEET POTATO CASSEROLE I

3 c. sweet potatoes, mashed (canned or fresh)
3/4 c. sugar
1/2 c. margarine
2 eggs, beaten
1 tsp. vanilla
1/2 c. milk

Mix all of the above together. Put in a 8 X 8 casserole dish.

Topping:

3/4-1 c. brown sugar
1/2 c. pecans, chopped
1/2 c. flour
1/3 c. margarine

Mix together to make crumbs. Sprinkle on top of potato mixture. Bake at 350 degrees for 25 minutes.

Yield: 10-12 servings

Nancy Kulp
Schuylkill Haven, PA

SWEET POTATO PATTIES

1 cold cooked sweet potato, mashed
1/2 c. bread crumbs or dry breakfast cereal, crushed

Shape cold mashed sweet potato into small patties. Roll in crumbs or cereal. Brown on both sides in a little fat.

For variety, add to the sweet potato chopped leftover meat, or finely chopped apple.

Yield: 2 servings

Mary Hille McCoy
Monterey, VA

SWEET POTATO APPLE SCALLOP II

3 large boiled sweet potatoes
2 c. pared sliced apples
3/4 c. sugar
1/4 c. melted butter
1/2 tsp. salt
dash of cinnamon, nutmeg and cloves
1/3 c. orange juice
grated rind of one orange

Peel potatoes, slice in 1/2-inch slices. Alternate layers of apples and potatoes in a greased baking dish. Mix sugar, rind, butter, salt, and spices into a paste. Spread over top of sweets and apples. Pour orange juice over mixture. Bake at 350 degrees in covered baking dish for 25 minutes, remove cover and continue baking another 20 minutes to brown top. Bake 45 minutes to 1 hour.

Yield: 8 servings

Betty Tongue
Lynchburg, VA

SWEET POTATOES IN ORANGE CUP

2 c. sweet potatoes cooked, and mashed
2 Tbsp. butter
1/2 tsp. salt
1/2 c. orange juice
3 large oranges
6 marshmallows, quartered

Combine sweet potatoes, butter, salt and orange juice. Mix well. Cut oranges in halves, crosswise, remove juice and pulp. Use part of juice when mashing potatoes. Scrub shells well. Fill with mashed potatoes and decorate with marshmallows. Bake at 400 degrees about 15 minutes. (Coconut or nuts may be added if desired)

Yield: 6 servings

Pauline Decker
Clarksville, VA

VEGETABLE CASSEROLE

yellow squash, sliced
onions, sliced
white potatoes, sliced
  (use as many vegetables as you like)
salt and pepper
margarine
Pepperidge Farm stuffing
Parmesan cheese

Fill casserole with layers of squash, onions and potatoes. Season with salt and pepper to taste. Dot with margarine. Cover and bake at 350 degrees until vegetables are tender. Cover with Pepperidge Farm stuffing, sprinkle with Parmesan cheese. Bake until brown.

Yield: as large a casserole as you like depending on number of vegetables used

Dorothy Blackard
Julian, NC

POTATOES IN CHICKEN-BROTH

1 1/2 lb. sliced potatoes (4 cups)
2 Tbsp. margarine
1 c. onion, sliced thinly
1 bay leaf
salt to taste
pepper to taste
1 1/2 c. chicken broth

Sauté onion in margarine. Add the remaining ingredients and bring to a simmer. Cover tightly and cook slowly, approximately 5 minutes. Then uncover and cook until liquid is absorbed.

Yield: 4-6 servings

Frances Robinson
Santa Fe, NM

SWEET POTATO CASSEROLE II

4 eggs
1 c. sugar
1/4 c. flour
2 tsp. vanilla
1 6 oz. can coconut
1 stick margarine
2 c. milk
1 large can sweet potatoes, mashed

Mix eggs, sugar, flour, and vanilla together. Add the remaining ingredients. Bake at 350 degrees for 50 to 60 minutes.

Yield: 10-12 servings

Leta Lester
Forest, VA

VIRGINIA SWEET POTATO PUDDING

2 eggs
1/2 c. sugar
2 Tbsp. white karo syrup
1 1/2 c. sweet potatoes, raw and grated
1/4 tsp. mace
1/4 tsp. ginger
1/4 tsp. cinnamon
1 tsp. vanilla
1 small can evaporated milk
1 c. sweet milk
1/4 c. butter, melted

Beat eggs lightly, add sugar and syrup, stir in potatoes and seasonings. Add milk and melted butter, blend. Bake 1 hour at 325 degrees.

Yield: 6 servings

Rosa L. Rizer
Clifton Forge, VA

notes

Main Dishes

notes

VENISON MEATBALLS

1 lb. lean venison, ground
1/4 lb. pork, ground
1 medium potato, ground
1 small onion, chopped
2 slices dry bread, crumbled
1 beaten egg, plus 2 Tbsp. evaporated milk
1 tsp. salt
1/4 tsp. sausage seasoning (optional)
1 tsp. prepared mustard
pepper to taste
1 tsp. Worcestershire sauce
1/4 c. salad oil

Mix all ingredients together. Shape into balls. Roll in flour and brown in hot oil. Lower heat and cook until done.

Yield: 30-36 meatballs

SALMON CROQUETTES

1 can salmon, drained
2 medium potatoes, peeled and diced
1 Tbsp. butter
1 egg, separated
3/4 c. bread crumbs
salt and pepper

Drain water from salmon. Remove bones and separate with fork. Boil the potatoes until tender. Drain and mash until free of lumps. While still hot add butter; season with salt and pepper. Beat the egg yolk and mix with the salmon and potatoes. Roll to desired size. Use the beaten egg white with 1 Tbsp. of cold water and dip the croquettes in this, then roll in bread crumbs and fry in shortening until brown.

Yield: 6-8 servings

Selene Stewart
Lynchburg, VA

STUFF

1 lb. ground beef
2-3 carrots, sliced thin
1-2 onions, sliced thin
2-3 potatoes, sliced thin
1/2 head cabbage, chopped
1 small can mushrooms
1 can cream of celery soup
Colby cheese, sliced

Press hamburger in bottom of a greased 9 X 13 casserole. Place the carrots in a layer on top of meat, then onions, potatoes, cabbage, mushrooms, top with cream of celery soup. Bake for 1-1 1/2 hours. Top with sliced cheese and heat until cheese is melted.

Yield: 6-8 servings

Mary Craddock
Manassas, VA

POTATO, HAM, AND CHEESE BAKE

2 lbs. potatoes, peeled and cut into 1 1/2 inch cubes
1 c. onion, chopped
1 c. sweet green pepper, chopped
1 Tbsp. vegetable oil
5 Tbsp. all-purpose flour
1/2 tsp. pepper
1/4 tsp. leaf thyme, crumbled
2 1/2 c. skim milk
1 c. sharp cheddar cheese, shredded
2 Tbsp. Dijon-style mustard
1 lb. bag frozen unthawed baby carrots
12 oz. turkey ham slices, cut into 2 x 1/2-inch strips
1/4 c. parsley, chopped

Cook potatoes in boiling water to cover in large saucepan for 10 minutes until fork-tender. Drain.

Cook onion and green pepper in oil in nonstick Dutch oven over medium heat until softened, 2-3 minutes. Stir in flour, pepper and thyme. Add milk. Bring to a boil. Lower heat; simmer, stirring until thickened, 2 minutes.

Stir in the mustard and all but one tablespoon of the cheddar cheese. Cook, stirring until cheese melts. Remove from heat. Gently fold in potatoes, carrots, ham, and parsley.   Pour into 4-quart casserole. Cover tightly with foil.

Bake in preheated hot oven (425 degrees) for 30 minutes. Sprinkle with reserved tablespoon of cheese. Bake uncovered for 5 minutes or until bubbly.

Yield: 8 servings

Nancy Kulp
Schuylkill Haven, PA

HAM 'N POTATO PIE

3 medium red potatoes
2 large onions
4 ham slices, boneless
1/2 tsp. salt
1/2 tsp. pepper

In shallow baking dish, make a layer of 1/4 inch thick potato slices overlapping each other. Slice onion thinly. Place half of it in rings over the potatoes. Sprinkle with salt and pepper. Over this layer place half of the ham that has been cut in pieces. Repeat layers of potatoes, onions, and ham. Sprinkle with remaining salt and pepper. Add enough water to reach ham. Bake uncovered at 350 degrees for about an hour.

Yield: 6-8 servings

Marilou Cross
Chattanooga, TN

CHOPPED MEAT AND POTATOES

1 lb. ground beef
3 medium onions, chopped
4 medium potatoes, diced*
1 green pepper, diced (optional)
2 Tbsp. vegetable oil
1/2 tsp. salt
1/4 tsp. pepper
1 c. water
1 28 oz. can tomato sauce
3/4 c. catsup

Brown meat, onions and pepper in oil. When meat is browned and onions are clear, add 1 c. of water and cook for 10 minutes. Add diced potatoes, salt, pepper, tomato sauce and catsup. Stir well. Add water, if necessary, in order to keep mixture from burning. Cook until potatoes are done. *More potatoes can be added if you have heavy eaters or need to stretch the meal.

Yield: 6-8 servings

Linda F. Chapman
Manassas, VA

POTATOES WITH SAUSAGE
(A MICROWAVE RECIPE)

4 medium or 2 large baking potatoes, slice in processor with
   peel on
1/4 c. water

Spread potatoes in pyrex dish, add water and cover with plastic wrap. Cook 7 minutes per pound. Turn dish halfway through cooking time. After potatoes are done, drain.

Combine:

1/2 tsp. salt
1 (3 oz. pkg.) cream cheese
1 Tbsp. flour
1/2 c. milk
2 tsp. chives
1/2 tsp. dry mustard

1/2 tsp. pepper
1/2 tsp. caraway seed (optional)
1 lb. polish sausage, fully cooked

To milk, add 1/2 tsp. salt, chives, dry mustard, pepper, caraway seed, flour, and mix this with softened cream cheese. Cook on full power 1-1 1/2 minutes to thicken. Pour sauce on top of potatoes, putting sliced sausage on top. Cover with plastic wrap. Cook 4-4 1/2 minutes on full power. Turn dish halfway through cooking time.

Yield: 6 servings

Mrs. Robert S. Estes
Marietta, GA

MEAT AND POTATO CASSEROLE

6 medium potatoes
3 Tbsp. butter
1 c. milk
1 tsp. salt
1 tsp. pepper
1 Tbsp. flour (if needed, for thickening)
2 Tbsp. onion, chopped
2 Tbsp. celery, chopped
5 slices American cheese or 1 c. Velveeta
1 lb. lean ground beef

Brown meat in skillet, drain off all fat. Turn heat to low, add chopped onions, celery, salt, pepper. Cook on low until celery and onions are tender. Meanwhile slice unpeeled scrubbed potatoes into cold salted water. Layer casserole dish (2 qt.) with beef mixture, sliced potatoes, slices of cheese, a little milk and dabs of butter. Have meat mixture as top layer. Cook at 350 degrees until potatoes are tender.

Yield: 6 servings

Alma LeNoir
Roanoke, VA

BAKED CRAB MEAT POTATOES

4 baking potatoes
1/2 c. light cream ·
1/2 medium onion, finely chopped
1 6 1/2-oz. can crab meat, drained
1 c. sharp Cheddar cheese, grated
1/2 c. softened butter
salt and pepper to taste

Bake potatoes. Halve and scoop out potato pulp. Mash pulp and add remaining ingredients; mix well. Refill potato skins and heat in 400 degree oven for 10 minutes, or until heated through.

Yield: 4 servings

Nancy Strachan
Bedford, VA

OVEN STEW

2 lb. chuck roast
2-3 onions
carrots
potatoes
salt & pepper
1 tsp. sugar
3 Tbsp. dry tapioca
1 c. tomato juice

Place the roast in a large baking dish or dutch oven. Slice 2 or 3 onions over roast. Top with carrots and potatoes. Add salt and pepper to taste and 1 tsp. sugar. Sprinkle with the tapioca. Pour tomato juice over all. (Thinned tomato soup also does well). Cover with tight fitting lid and bake in 275 degree oven for four hours without removing lid.

Yield: 4-6 servings

Susan Layne
Bedford, VA

There is enough for all. The earth is a generous mother; she will provide in plentiful abundance food for all her children if they will but cultivate her soil in justice and in peace.
                                                        -Bourke Cockran

BREAKFAST PIZZA

1 pkg. refrigerated crescent rolls
1 lb. bulk sausage
1 c. frozen hash brown potatoes
1 c. cheddar cheese (grated)
5 eggs
1/2 tsp. salt
1/4 tsp. pepper
1/4 c. milk

Spread rolls on pizza pan. Brown sausage and drain. Combine sausage, hash brown potatoes, and cheese, along with the eggs beaten with the salt, pepper and milk. Pour into crust. Bake at 375 degrees for 25 minutes.

Yield: 4 servings

Pat Heilman
Austin, TX

BEEF POTATO BAKE

1/2 lb. ground chuck beef or 1 c. diced cooked beef
1 c. minced onion
1 Tbsp. oil
1/8 tsp. pepper
2 tsp. salt
1/4 tsp. each: thyme, sage, marjoram
2 slices very stale bread
cold water
2 1/2 c. grated raw white potatoes
1 c. milk
2 eggs, beaten

Heat oven to 400 degrees. Sauté beef and onion in oil in skillet until meat has lost all red. Remove from heat; add next five ingredients. Soak bread in cold water to cover until soft; squeeze out water and put into greased 1 1/2-qt. casserole. Bake covered at 400 degrees for 1 hour. Uncover and bake 5 minutes longer, or until nicely browned. A good way to use leftovers.

Yield: 4 large servings

Ann McAlister
Lynchburg, VA

CORNED BEEF AND CABBAGE CASSEROLE

5 med. size potatoes (sliced thinly)
1 small onion (chopped)
1 tsp. salt
4 c. shredded cabbage
1 can cream of celery soup
1/2 tsp. pepper
1 can corned beef (12 oz.)
1 1/2 c. milk

Place sliced potatoes in a shallow pan or baking dish, 13 X 9.

Cover with onions, salt and pepper, add shredded cabbage, crumble corned beef and spoon it over the cabbage. Cover with cream of celery soup diluted with the milk. Cover and bake. Set oven 375 degrees for 1 1/2 hrs.

Yield: 6-8 servings

Rosa L. Rizer
Clifton Forge, VA

POTATO WIENER CASSEROLE

7 medium white potatoes, cooked until tender
1 pkg. wieners
1/2 c. flour
1 c. milk
salt and pepper to taste
butter

Slice potatoes 1/4 inch thick. Arrange in 2-qt. casserole in layers with salt, pepper, butter and sprinkle of flour. Add layers of wieners. Continue layers until all used up. Pour milk over all. Bake in 350 degree oven until bubbly and browned.

Yield: 4-6 servings

Mary Quick
Lynchburg, VA

"As common a vegetable as is the potato, no two cooks are agreed in the best manner of cooking it."
- A Married Lady, The Improved Housewife, 1845

RED SNAPPER BAKED WITH POTATOES

2 2 lb. red snappers, cleaned but with heads and tails left on,
    or substitute any firm white fish
1 1/2 tsp. salt
1 lemon, cut into 6 wedges
2 small black olives
3/4 c. soft crumbs made from French or Italian bread
1 tsp. finely chopped garlic
1 Tbsp. finely chopped parsley
2 Tbsp. paprika
3 medium-size boiling potatoes, peeled and cut into 1/4-inch
    rounds
freshly ground black pepper
1 c. water
1/2 c. olive oil

Preheat the oven to 350 degrees. Wash the fish under cold
running water and pat them dry, inside and out, with paper
towels. Sprinkle the fish with 1 tsp. of the salt, then place them
side by side on a board or plate.

With a small, sharp knife, score each fish, making three cross-
wise parallel cuts about 1/4 inch deep, 2 inches long and 1 1/2
inches apart. Insert a wedge of lemon, skin side up, in each
cut. Insert a black olive in the exposed eye socket of each fish.

In a small bowl, combine the bread crumbs, garlic, parsley and
paprika. Spread the potato slices evenly on the bottom of a 16
X 10-inch baking dish. Sprinkle them with the remaining 1/2
tsp. of salt and a few grindings of pepper and place the fish side
by side on top. Pour the water down the side of the baking dish
and pour the olive oil over the fish. Sprinkle them evenly with
the bread-crumb mixture.

Bake in the middle of the oven for 30 minutes, or until the fish
feels firm when pressed lightly with a finger and the potatoes
beneath them are done. Serve at once, directly from the baking
dish.

Yield: 4-6 servings

Jean K. Horne
Bedford, VA

SCALLOPED POTATOES WITH SALAMI SLICES

1/4 c. butter
1/4 c. flour
1/2 tsp. salt
1/4 tsp. pepper
3 c. milk
1/2 lb. thinly sliced salami
4 c. thinly sliced potatoes
1 med. onion, thinly sliced

Melt the butter in a saucepan over low heat and blend in flour and seasonings. Add the milk slowly and cook, stirring constantly, until smooth and thickened. Cut the salami slices in quarters. Arrange alternate layers of potatoes, onion, salami, and white sauce in a greased 2-qt. casserole and cover the casserole. Bake at 350 degrees for 40 minutes. Remove cover and bake for 20 to 30 minutes longer or until potatoes are tender and top is brown.

Yield: 6 servings

LUNCHEON MEAT-BROCCOLI DISH

2 12-oz. cans luncheon meat (Spam)
prepared mustard
2 pkgs. frozen broccoli spears
2 c. mashed potatoes
2 Tbsp. margarine

Cut each can of luncheon meat into 3 slices and place in a 2-qt. baking dish. Spread with mustard. Thaw the broccoli and place over luncheon meat. Top with potatoes and dot with margarine. Bake in 350 degree oven for 35 minutes or until potatoes are brown.

Yield: 6 servings

SAVORY POTATO CHILI

1 lb. ground beef
1/2 c. chopped onion
1/2 c. chopped green pepper
1 Tbsp. poppy seeds
1/2 tsp. salt
1/2 tsp. chili powder
1 (5.25-oz.) pkg. scalloped potato mix
1 c. hot water
1 (16-oz.) kidney beans, undrained
1 (16-oz.) can whole tomatoes, undrained and chopped
1 (4-oz.) can mushroom stems and pieces, undrained
          grated Parmesan cheese

Combine ground beef, onion, and green pepper in a large skillet; cook over medium heat until beef is browned, stirring to crumble meat. Drain off drippings. Stir in remaining ingredients, except cheese, mixing well. Cover, reduce heat, and simmer 45 minutes or until liquid is absorbed, stirring occasionally. Sprinkle each serving with Parmesan cheese.

Yield: 6 servings

CREAMED BEEF AND CHICKEN-TOPPED POTATOES

4 large baking potatoes
vegetable oil
3 Tbsp. butter
1/4 c. finely chopped onion
2 Tbsp. minced celery
1 (2 1/2-oz.) jar sliced dried beef, finely chopped
3 1/2 Tbsp. all-purpose flour
2 c. milk
1/2 c. diced cooked chicken
1 tsp. lemon juice
1 tsp. Worcestershire sauce
1/4 tsp. dried whole thyme
1/8 tsp. pepper

Wash potatoes, and rub with oil. Bake at 400 degrees for 1 hour or until done.

Melt butter in a medium saucepan; add onion, celery, and dried beef; cook until onion is tender. Stir in flour; cook 1 minute, stirring constantly. Gradually add milk; cook over medium heat, stirring constantly, until sauce is thickened and bubbly. Stir in next 5 ingredients, and cook until mixture is thoroughly heated.

Split tops of potatoes, lengthwise, and fluff pulp with a fork. Spoon topping over potatoes.

Yield: 4 servings

EASY POTATO PANCAKES AND SAUSAGES

1 egg
3/4 c. pancake mix
1 c. milk
1 Tbsp. vegetable oil
3 med. potatoes, peeled, and grated
1 med. onion, grated
1 (8-oz.) pkg. frozen brown 'n' serve sausages
applesauce

Beat egg in medium bowl, stir in pancake mix, milk, oil, potatoes, onion, stir until fairly smooth. Heat lightly greased skillet or griddle, use 1/4 c. batter for each pancake. Fry to a golden brown, about 4 minutes per side. Serve with applesauce and sausages.

Yield: 4-6 servings

POTATOES AND CHICKEN STIR-FRY

2 medium potatoes, boiled and cut in cubes
1 lb. chicken breast cut in strips
2 Tbsp. soy sauce
1 Tbsp. cornstarch
2 Tbsp. oil
1 large onion, sliced
2 cloves garlic, minced
3/4 tsp. ground ginger
1/4 c. broth or water
2 tomatoes, cut in wedges

Combine soy sauce, cornstarch, and toss with chicken strips. Heat oil in wok, add onion and garlic and brown slightly, add potatoes. Cook until brown. Add chicken strips and cook approximately 4 minutes. Add broth and cook an additional 2 minutes. Stir in tomatoes, cook for 1 minute.

Yield: 4 servings

RABBIT STEW

1 rabbit (3 to 4 lbs.)
4 Tbsp. olive oil
2 med. onions, chopped
1 No. 2 can tomatoes
1 c. water
3-4 medium potatoes
salt and pepper to taste
1/8 tsp. crushed red pepper

Have rabbit cleaned and cut into serving pieces. Place in enamel pot. Cover with water to which 2 Tbsp. of salt have been added. Let it stand for 2 hours, then wash in cold running water and dry with absorbent paper. Heat oil in pot. Sauté rabbit and onion for about 20 minutes. Season with salt and pepper; continue browning. Add tomatoes. Cover tightly; cook slowly for about 20 min. Add quartered potatoes and 1 c. of water. Continue cooking 1/2 hour longer or until rabbit and potatoes are tender.

Yield: 4-6 servings

Jean K. Horne
Bedford, VA

POTATO PAPRIKA

2 lbs. boiling potatoes
1/3 tsp. caraway seeds
1 med.-size tomato, peeled, seeded, and chopped (about 1/4 c.)
3 Tbsp. lard
2/3 c. finely chopped onions
1 large green pepper with seeds and ribs removed, finely chopped
1/4 tsp. finely chopped garlic
1 Tbsp. sweet Hungarian paprika
1 tsp. salt
freshly ground black pepper
2 c. chicken or beef stock, fresh or canned, or 2 c. water
1 lb. Hungarian sausage
1/2 c. sour cream

Cook the potatoes in boiling water for 8 to 10 minutes, then peel and cut into 1/4-inch slices. In a 4-quart saucepan or casserole, heat the lard until a light haze forms over it, then add the onions and garlic. Cook for 8 to 10 minutes, or until lightly colored. Turn off the heat, stir in paprika. Stir until the onions are well coated. Return the pan to the heat, add stock or water, bring to a boil, and add caraway seeds, potatoes, tomato, green pepper, salt and a few grindings of pepper. Bring the liquid to a boil, stir, cover and simmer for 25 to 30 minutes until the potatoes are tender.

The addition of the smoked sausage to potato paprika makes the dish a complete meal. Slice the sausage about 1/8 inch thick and add it when you add the potatoes.

Top with sour cream when ready to serve.

Yield: 4-6 servings

Jean K. Horne
Bedford, VA

SPANISH GREEN BEAN AND POTATO FRITTATA

2 Tbsp. olive oil
1 c. diced onion
1 garlic clove, minced
3 c. diced cooked potatoes
2 c. diced cooked green beans
1 c. diced cooked carrots
1 tsp. oregano
1/2 tsp. thyme
4 eggs, beaten
2/3 c. milk
1 1/2 c. grated cheddar cheese

Heat oil in a medium frying pan. Cook the onions and garlic until clear, about five minutes. Add the oregano and thyme. Mix in the beans, carrots and potatoes.

In a separate bowl, beat the eggs until yellow and add the milk. Mix well. Pour the egg mixture into a greased 9 X 13-inch baking dish. Spoon the vegetable mixture in and distribute evenly. Sprinkle cheese on top. Bake at 350 degrees for one hour or until it is set.

Yield: 6-8 servings

CRUSTLESS POTATO QUICHE

5 eggs, beaten
1 (12-oz.) pkg. frozen hash brown potatoes, thawed
1 c. shredded Swiss cheese
1 large green onion, chopped
1/2 c. cream-style cottage cheese
1/4 tsp. salt
1/8 tsp. pepper
dash of hot sauce
paprika
6 slices bacon, cooked & crumbled

Combine first 8 ingredients; stir well. Pour mixture into a

lightly greased 9-inch pie plate; sprinkle with paprika. Bake at 350 degrees for 25 minutes or until set. Sprinkle bacon evenly on top; bake an additional 5 minutes. Let stand 5 minutes before serving.

Yield: 1 9-inch pie

TUNA-POTATO SCALLOP

1 pkg. (5.5 oz.) scalloped potatoes
1 can (9 1/4 oz.) tuna, drained
1 can (10 1/2 oz.) condensed cream of celery soup
2 Tbsp. chopped pimento

Heat oven to 400 degrees. Empty potato slices into ungreased 2-qt. casserole; sprinkle with packet of sauce mix. Stir in amount of boiling water as directed on package, the tuna, soup and pimento. Bake uncovered 35 to 40 minutes.

Yield: 4-6 servings.

Laura Newell-Furniss
Lynchburg, VA

POTATO SCRAMBLE

6 slices bacon, diced
2 c. diced cooked potatoes
1 med. onion, diced
1 tsp. salt
1/4 tsp. pepper
4 eggs, beaten

Fry bacon until crisp, drain off all but 3 Tbsp. fat. Cook and stir potatoes, onion, salt and pepper in fat until light brown. Pour eggs into skillet. Cook uncovered until eggs are thickened.

Yield: 4 servings

WAYNE'S POTATO, HAM & CABBAGE

1 6-8 pound picnic ham
8 medium potatoes, pared and cubed
1 pound cabbage, cut into wedge shaped pieces
pepper to taste

Trim the skin off the ham. Cover the ham with water. Boil until you can pull the meat apart with a fork. Remove the ham and all the broth except enough to cook the potatoes in. Cube about 1 - 1 1/2 pounds of the ham to use for this recipe (you can use fat, small bones etc. they provide good flavor but are not necessarily healthy). Slice the rest of the ham to use for other meals. (The large ham bone is good for making soupbeans, etc.)

Add the potatoes and the cubed ham to the broth that you left in the pot. Cover with a lid and cook for 15 minutes then add the cabbage, making a solid layer, add pepper, cover and cook for another 5 minutes depending on how cooked you like your cabbage.

Yield: 4-6 servings

Wayne Newell
Lynchburg, VA

MEAT POTATO QUICHE

3 Tbsp. oil
3 c. coarsely shredded raw potatoes
1 c. grated swiss or cheddar cheese
3/4 c. cooked chicken, ham, or brown sausage, diced
1/4 c. onions, chopped
1 c. evaporated milk or rich milk
2 eggs
1/2 tsp. salt
1/8 tsp. pepper
1 Tbsp. parsley flakes

Stir together the oil and potatoes in a 9-inch pie pan. Press evenly into the pan to form a crust. Bake at 425 degrees for 15 minutes, until it is just beginning to brown. Remove from the oven.

Add the cheese, meat, and onions to the potato crust.

Beat together the milk, eggs, salt, and pepper in a bowl. Pour the egg mixture over the other ingredients in the potato crust. Sprinkle the parsley flakes on top. Return to oven and bake at 425 degrees for about 30 minutes or until lightly brown. Allow to cool 5 minutes before cutting into wedges.

Yield: 4-6 servings

Faye Everett
Millington, MD

DORANDO'S MOCK LASAGNA

1 c. mashed potatoes (or cook one large potato and mash with a
    small amount of milk)
1/4 lb. ground beef
1/2 c. tomato sauce
2 1/2-oz. mushrooms, drained, or 1/2 c. fresh mushrooms,
    sliced
1/2 c. cottage cheese
1/4 lb. Monterey Jack cheese, sliced
2 Tbsp. grated Parmesan cheese

Spread mashed potatoes in a 1-qt. casserole. Brown ground beef and drain fat. Stir in tomato sauce and mushrooms. Spread cottage cheese over mashed potatoes; top with meat sauce. Cover with cheese slices and sprinkle with Parmesan cheese. Bake at 350 degrees for 35 to 40 minutes.

Yield: 2-3 servings

Joanne Milkereit
Charleston, SC

VEGETARIAN TACO FILLING

3 Tbsp. vegetable oil
1 clove garlic, minced
1 medium onion, finely chopped
1 bell pepper, finely chopped
2-3 large potatoes, or 1-2 medium sweet potatoes, or 2-3 large
    carrots, 1 large eggplant, zucchini or yellow (summer)
    squash (or 1 small one of each)
4-6 medium tomatoes or 1 15-oz. can of tomatoes
1 c. cooked lentils or beans, or 1 15-oz. can of beans
1 c. water (more or less)

Gently sauté first three ingredients in the oil. Meanwhile, chop
potatoes, sweet potatoes, or whatever vegetable you chose, into
small cubes. When onion and pepper are soft, add taco seasoning (recipe is below, or use 1 pkg. prepared taco seasoning).
Then add chopped vegetables, tossing lightly so all are covered
with spices. Add water. Cover and cook over medium heat
until all are soft. In the meantime, peel and chop tomatoes (or
use canned, chopped tomatoes, reserving juice). When vegetables are all soft, add chopped tomatoes. If it is soupy, remove
lid and turn up heat. If it is dry, add water or reserved tomato
juice. Add lentils or beans at this point. When they are hot
through, use potato masher to blend vegetable mixture. Adjust
seasoning and serve in crisp taco shells with shredded lettuce,
chopped tomatoes, chopped onions and cucumbers, black
olives, taco sauce and sour cream.

VEGETARIAN TACO SEASONING MIX

1 Tbsp. chili powder
1 tsp. cumin
1/2 tsp. salt
1/2 tsp. crushed hot red pepper flakes or
    1-2 chili peppers (fresh or dried)
1/2 tsp. oregano

Mix the above together.

If using with beef tacos, add:

1 medium onion, minced
1 clove garlic, minced
1 medium green pepper, minced

Variation:
1 Tbsp. instant minced onion
1/2 tsp. instant minced garlic

Yield: 6 servings

Patsy Martin
Big Island, VA

'If you ate only potatoes you'd consume 10 times the amount of vitamin C, one and a half times the iron, all the riboflavin, and three to four times the thiamin and niacin the body needs.'
-U.S. Department of Agriculture.

POTATO-TOPPED LUNCHEON MEAT

1 can luncheon meat, sliced
3 c. mashed potatoes
2 Tbsp. minced green onion
1/4 c. stuffed olives, chopped
1 Tbsp. parsley, chopped
dash of pepper
paprika

Place meat in shallow casserole. Combine potatoes with remaining ingredients except paprika; moisten with a little milk if necessary. Mix well. Spread on meat. Sprinkle with paprika. Bake in preheated oven of 350 degrees for 35 minutes.

Yield: 4 servings

POTATO TAMALES WITH BELL PEPPER

1 lb. boiling potatoes, cooked until tender
13 Tbsp. butter, softened
1 1/3 c. instant masa mix
2 tsp. achiote paste (available in Latin American markets)
1/2 tsp. salt
1/2 tsp. cinnamon
1/2 tsp. ground cloves
1/2 tsp. red chili powder
1 lb. ripe tomatoes, chopped
1 c. pimentos or red bell peppers, chopped
1/2 large onion, chopped
1/2 c. water
4 garlic cloves
1 small pasilla chili (dark brown dried chili available in Latin
   American markets)
1 green bell pepper, chopped
2 Tbsp. fresh parsley, chopped
8 corn husks, softened in hot water

Peel potatoes. Work through fine plate of food mill or sieve into
bowl. Add 10 Tbsp. butter and next 6 ingredients and stir until
smooth.

Combine next 6 ingredients in heavy large saucepan over medium-
high heat and cook until pastelike, stirring frequently about 30
minutes. Purée in blender or processor. Strain into potato mixture
and stir to blend.

Melt remaining 3 Tbsp. butter in heavy medium skillet over
medium-high heat. Add green pepper and sauté until crisp-
tender, about 5 minutes. Add to potato mixture. Stir in parsley.

Place 1/4 c. mixture in center of each husk. Fold in sides, then
ends. Arrange seam side down on rack in steamer. Cover and
steam over high heat until filling is solid, 30 minutes.

Yield: 8 tamales

Nancy Spivey
Houston, TX

Breads & Desserts

notes

POTATO ROLLS

1 pkg. dry yeast
3 3/4 c. flour
1/4 c. sugar
1 tsp. salt
1 egg
1 potato, small
1/4 c. shortening
oleo

Cut potato in small pieces.   Cook in small amount of water, about 1 cup.   When potato is done, strain both the potato and water.   To this add enough cold water to potato water to make 1 1/2 cups.   Break egg into this and beat until mixed with water.   Add yeast while water is still warm.   Sift flour, sugar and salt in mixing bowl.   Work in shortening.   Add first mixture and mix by hand until dough is good consistency to handle.   Knead until supple and springs back.   Put in greased bowl, grease top of dough and put in warm place to rise (3 hours).   Make into rolls and grease with half oleo and half shortening, melted.   Let rise 1 hour.   Cook at 425 degrees about 10-12 minutes.

Yield: 2 dozen

Selene Stewart
Lynchburg, VA

SWEET POTATO BISCUITS

2 c. sweet potatoes, mashed
9 Tbsp. shortening, melted (butter is best)
1/3 c. milk
2 1/2 c. flour, sifted
4 Tbsp. sugar
1 tsp. baking powder
1 tsp. salt

Add melted butter to potatoes, then add milk and sugar then flour which has been sifted with salt and baking powder.   Pat or roll to 1/2 inch thickness.   Cut with floured cutter.   Bake at 450 degrees for 15 to 20 minutes.

Yield: 2 dozen

POTATO YEAST*

4 c. potatoes, peeled and cubed
1 pkg. dry yeast
2 c. warm water, divided
1/4 c. sugar
1 1/2 tsp. salt

Cook potatoes in boiling water to cover for 10 minutes or until tender; drain. Mash potatoes and let cool. Dissolve yeast in 1/2 cup warm water; let stand 5 minutes. Combine yeast mixture, sugar, salt, and potatoes in a medium-size nonmetal bowl; stir well. Add remaining 1 1/2 cups water and stir well. Cover loosely with plastic wrap, and let stand in a warm place (80-85 degrees) for 72 hours, stirring 2 or 3 times daily. Place fermented mixture in refrigerator 24 hours before making Potato Yeast Rolls.

To use, remove potato yeast from refrigerator, and let stand at room temperature at least 1 hour.

Yield: 4 cups

Yeast mixture will keep in refrigerator up to 14 days, stir daily.

POTATO YEAST ROLLS

1/3 c. milk, scalded
3 Tbsp. shortening
2 Tbsp. sugar
1 tsp. salt
1 c. potato yeast*
1 egg, beaten
3-3 1/2 c. all purpose flour, divided

Combine first 4 ingredients; stir until sugar dissolves. Cool to lukewarm. Add potato yeast, egg and 1 1/2 cups flour; beat at medium speed in electric mixer until smooth. Stir in enough remaining flour to make a soft dough.

Turn dough out onto a floured surface and knead until smooth and elastic (about 5 minutes). Place in a well greased bowl, turning to grease top. Cover and let rise in a warm place free of drafts, 1 1/2 hours or until doubled in bulk. Punch dough down, shape into 2-inch balls. Place in a greased 13 X 9-inch pan. Cover and let rise in a warm place 1 hour or until doubled in bulk. Bake at 400 degrees for 15 to 17 minutes or until golden.

Yield: 2 dozen

POTATO GARLIC BISCUITS

1/2 lb. red potatoes, peeled and quartered
2-4 large garlic cloves, whole and peeled
1/3 c. butter or margarine, softened
1/2 tsp. salt
1/4 tsp. pepper
2 c. flour
2 Tbsp. baking powder
1/3 c. milk, cold

Cover potatoes and garlic with water, cook until tender, 20-25 minutes. Drain; mash potato and garlic in bowl. Stir in butter or margarine, salt and pepper. In another bowl sift flour and baking powder together. Stir into potato mixture. Stir in milk. Form into a ball. Roll out on lightly floured surface to 1/2 inch thickness. Cut into 2-inch rounds and arrange on ungreased baking sheet 1 inch apart. Bake in 450 degree oven 8 to 10 minutes until risen but not browned. Cool on rack. Put into freezer bags. Press out air and freeze. When ready to serve, bake frozen biscuits in 450 degree oven about 10 minutes until lightly browned. Serve warm.

Yield: 1 dozen

He who has nothing to boast of, but his ancestors is like a potato - the best of him is underground.

- Pioneer Proverbs

SWEET POTATO MUFFINS

1/2 c. butter
1 1/2 c. sugar
2 eggs
1 1/4 c. sweet potatoes, cooked and mashed
  (canned sweet potatoes may be used)
1 1/2 c. all-purpose flour
2 tsp. baking powder
1/4 tsp. salt
1 tsp. cinnamon
1/4 tsp. nutmeg
1 c. milk
1/4 c. pecans or walnuts
1/2 c. raisins

Cream butter, sugar and eggs. Mix well. Blend in the sweet potatoes. Sift flour with baking powder, salt, cinnamon and nutmeg. Add to creamed mixture alternately with milk. Do not overmix. Fold in nuts and raisins. Fill greased muffin tins 2/3 full. Bake at 400 degrees for 25 minutes. Muffins freeze well.

Yield: 3 doz.

Pauline Decker
Clarksville, VA

POTATO REFRIGERATOR ROLLS

1 pkg. dry yeast
1/2 c. water (potato water)
2/3 c. shortening
1/2 c. sugar
1 c. mashed potatoes
1 c. milk
2 eggs
6-8 c. flour, sifted
2 tsp. salt

To warm mashed potatoes, add salt, shortening, sugar and eggs. Blend well. Dissolve yeast in lukewarm potato water. Add to milk, then to potato mixture. Add sifted flour to make a stiff dough. Knead well. Place in greased bowl and allow to rise to twice its size.   Punch down.   Rub with butter or shortening and put in covered container.   Place in refrigerator for 2 hours before making into rolls.   (Will keep for several days at this stage)   Pinch off balls of dough and make rolls into desired size and shape.   Let rise again.   Bake in 400 degree oven for about 15 minutes, or until golden brown.

Yield: 2 1/2-3 dozen

Susan G. Carden
Cumberland, VA

WILLIAMSBURG SWEET POTATO MUFFINS

2/3 c. canned or fresh cooked sweet potatoes, drained well
4 Tbsp. butter
1/2 c. sugar
1 egg
3/4 c. all-purpose flour
2 tsp. baking powder
1/2 tsp. salt
1/2 tsp. cinnamon
1/4 tsp. nutmeg
1/2 c. milk
4 Tbsp. walnuts or pecans, chopped
4 Tbsp. raisins, chopped

Preheat oven to 400 degrees.   Grease muffin tins.

Purée the sweet potatoes in a food processor or blender. Cream the butter and sugar.   Beat in the egg and sweet potatoes.   Sift the flour with the baking powder, salt, cinnamon, and nutmeg. Add the dry ingredients alternately by hand with the milk, chopped nuts and raisins, mixing just until blended. Don't overmix.

Spoon into the greased muffin tins, filling each tin completely full.   You may sprinkle a little sugar and cinnamon on top of each muffin before baking. Bake at 400 degrees for 25 minutes.

Yield: 1 1/2 dozen

Margie Anderson
Big Island, VA

GOLDEN ROLLS

1 c. milk, scalded
1/4 c. water
1/2 c. margarine
1/3 c. sugar
2 yeast cakes
1 c. mashed sweet potatoes
1 1/2 tsp. salt
1 c. flour
2 eggs, beaten
4-5 c. additional flour

Scald milk. Mix yeast with lukewarm water. Mix the hot milk, fat, and sugar, stir in the mashed potatoes and let stand until mixture is lukewarm. Add 1 cup flour and beaten eggs. Stir yeast and add to mixture. Beat until ingredients are thoroughly mixed. Cover and set aside in warm place until mixture is risen and full of bubbles. Add more flour, enough to make the dough stiff. Knead until dough is elastic. Store in refrigerator or let dough rise until it is doubled in size. Shape into rolls. Let rise until they are at least 2 1/2 times their size. Bake at 400 degrees for 20-25 minutes.

Yield: 4 dozen

Mary Hille McCoy
Monterey, VA

HONEY WHOLE WHEAT BREAD

2 pkgs. active dry yeast
5 c. warm water
6 Tbsp. shortening
1/4 c. honey
4 c. whole wheat flour
1/2 c. instant potatoes (not reconstituted)
1/2 c. nonfat dry milk
1 Tbsp. salt
6 1/2 to 8 c. sifted all-purpose flour

Sprinkle yeast on 1/2 c. warm water; stir to dissolve. Melt shortening in 6-qt. saucepan; remove from heat, add honey and remaining 4 1/2 c. warm water.

Mix whole wheat flour (stirred before measuring), instant potatoes, dry milk and salt. Add to saucepan; beat until smooth. Add yeast and beat to blend. Then with wooden spoon mix in enough all-purpose flour, a little at a time, to make a dough that leaves the sides of the pan. Turn onto lightly floured board and knead until smooth and small bubbles appear, 8 to 10 minutes.

Place in lightly greased bowl; turn dough over to grease top. Cover and let rise in warm place until doubled, 1 to 1 1/2 hrs. Punch down dough, turn onto board and divide in thirds. Cover and let rest 5 minutes. Shape into 3 loaves and place in greased 9 X 5 loaf pans. Cover and let rise until doubled, about 1 hr.

Bake in hot oven (400 degrees) about 50 minutes or until bread tests done. Remove from the pans and cool.

Note: 1 c. mashed potatoes may be used in place of the instant potatoes. Combine with the honey-water mixture.

Yield: 3 loaves

Jean K. Horne
Bedford, VA

> And the King will answer them, "Truly, I say to you, as you did it to one of the least of these my brethren, you did it to me."
> Matthew 25:40

ROADSIDE POTATO BREAD

3 1/2 c. milk
6 Tbsp. sugar
6 Tbsp. butter
2 tsp. salt
1/4 c. instant mashed potatoes (not reconstituted)
2 pkgs. active dry yeast
1/2 c. warm water
10 to 11 c. sifted all-purpose flour
3 Tbsp. cornmeal

Scald milk; pour into large bowl and stir in sugar, butter, salt and instant mashed potatoes. Cool to lukewarm. Sprinkle yeast on warm water; stir to dissolve. Add yeast and 4 c. flour to milk mixture. Beat 2 minutes with electric mixer at medium speed, or until batter is smooth. Or beat by hand. Mix in just enough of remaining flour, a little at a time, first with spoon and then with hands to make a dough that leaves the sides of bowl.

Turn onto lightly floured board; cover and let rest 10 to 15 minutes. Knead until smooth, about 10 minutes. Place in greased bowl; turn dough over to grease top. Cover and let rise in warm place until doubled; 1 1/2 to 2 hours. Punch down dough; cover and let rise again until doubled, about 45 minutes.

Turn onto board and divide in 3 equal parts; round up in balls, cover and let rest 10 minutes. Meanwhile, grease 3 loaf pans. Sprinkle bottoms and sides of pans with cornmeal (1 Tbsp. to each pan).

Shape dough into loaves; place in pans, cover and let rise until doubled, 50 to 60 minutes. Bake at 375 degrees for 45 minutes or until loaves are brown and have a hollow sound when tapped with fingers. Remove from pans and cool.

Yield: 3 loaves

Jean K. Horne
Bedford, VA

122

POTATO PUFF ROLLS

1/2 c. mashed potatoes, made from instant mashed potatoes,
 unseasoned
1 c. milk
1/4 c. shortening
1/4 c. sugar
1 tsp. salt
1 pkg. active dry yeast
1/4 c. warm water
4-4 1/2 c. sifted all-purpose flour
1 egg

Scald milk. Add shortening, sugar, salt and potatoes. Cool to
lukewarm. Sprinkle yeast on warm water; stir to dissolve.
Combine milk mixture, yeast, 2 c. flour and egg. Beat well by
hand or with electric mixer at medium speed, scraping the
bowl occasionally, to make smooth mixture, about 2 minutes.
Stir in enough remaining flour, a little at time, to make a soft
dough that leaves the sides of the bowl.

Turn onto lightly floured board and knead until satiny and
elastic, 5 to 10 minutes. Place in lightly greased bowl; turn
dough over to grease top. Cover and let rise in warm place until
doubled, 1 to 1 1/2 hrs. Punch down.

Turn onto board. Shape into a ball, cover and let rest 10 minutes. Pinch off small pieces of dough and shape in balls to half
fill greased muffin-pan cups. Cover and let rise until almost
doubled, about 1 hr.

Bake in 400 degree oven 10 to 12 minutes.

Yield: 34 rolls

POTATO DOUGHNUTS

1 3/4 c. milk
1/2 c. shortening
1/2 c. sugar
1/2 c. mashed potatoes
1 pkg. active dry yeast
1/2 c. warm water
2 eggs, beaten
1/2 tsp. vanilla
6 1/2 to 7 c. sifted all-purpose flour
1 tsp. baking powder
1 tsp. salt

Thin glaze:
confectioners' sugar
milk

Scald milk; stir in shortening, sugar and mashed potatoes.
Cool to lukewarm. Blend well.

Sprinkle yeast over warm water and stir until yeast is dissolved.
Add to milk mixture. Stir in beaten eggs and vanilla.

Sift 6 1/2 c. flour with baking powder and salt; add gradually to
yeast mixture, mixing well after each addition. Add another 1/2
c. flour if needed to make a soft dough you can handle (use no
more than necessary). Turn into greased bowl; turn dough over
to grease top. Cover and let rise in warm place until doubled,
about 1 1/2 hrs.

Roll to 1/2 in. thickness on floured board. Cut with floured
doughnut cutter, reserving centers to make Pecan Rolls (recipe
follows). Place cut-out doughnuts on waxed paper; cover with
cloth and let rise in warm place until doubled, about 30 minutes. Fry a few doughnuts at a time in hot vegetable oil (375
degrees). Drain on absorbent paper. Spread warm doughnuts
with a thin glaze made of confectioners' sugar and milk, or
shake them in a bag containing sugar to coat them.

Yield: 4 dozen doughnuts

PECAN ROLLS FROM POTATO DOUGHNUT CENTERS

12 tsp. brown sugar
12 tsp. light corn syrup
6 tsp. water
36 pecan halves
48 raisins
doughnut centers leftover from doughnuts

Lightly grease 12 medium-size muffin-pan cups. In the bottom of each cup, place 1 tsp. brown sugar, 1 tsp. corn syrup, 1/2 tsp. water, 3 pecan halves and 4 raisins. Arrange 4 doughnut centers on top, cover with cloth and let rise in warm place until doubled, about 30 minutes. Bake in 350 degree oven 25 to 30 minutes.

Yield: 12 rolls

POTATO BISCUITS

3/4 c. shortening
1/2 c. sugar
1 c. hot riced potatoes
1 1/2 tsp. salt
1 c. milk
1 yeast cake dissolved in 1/4 c. lukewarm water
2 egg yolks, beaten
2 egg whites, beaten
Flour (5 1/2 c.)

Combine shortening, sugar, potatoes, salt, milk, 1 c. flour, dissolved yeast cake, and eggs. Cover, let rise until light. Add 4 1/2 c. flour, cover, and again let rise. Turn onto floured board, pat, and roll 1/4 inch thick. Shape with small round cutter. Put together in pairs with butter between the layers. Let rise and bake in hot oven at 425 degrees.

Yield: 30-36 biscuits

Ruth Smith Newell

POTATO BREAD

2 c. potato water*
1 cake compressed yeast
2 Tbsp. shortening
2 Tbsp. sugar
1 Tbsp. salt
6 - 6 1/2 c. sifted flour

Heat potato water to lukewarm. Crumble yeast in 1/4 c. of the liquid. To the remaining liquid, add shortening, sugar and salt. Add softened yeast and 1/2 of the flour. Beat; add remaining flour gradually. Toss on floured board and knead until thoroughly elastic. Place in a bowl, cover and let rise. When double in bulk, divide into 2 parts, shape into loaves and place in greased pans. Let rise again until dough has doubled in bulk. Bake in a moderately hot oven (375 degrees) for 45 minutes or until bread shrinks from sides of pan.

Yield: 2 1-lb. loaves

*Potato Water: Cook 3 peeled potatoes until tender; mash in liquid.

ONION CHEESE BRAID

1 pkg. active dry yeast
1/2 c. warm water
1/2 tsp. sugar
3/4 c. milk
1/2 c. unseasoned mashed potatoes
1/4 c. margarine
1 Tbsp. sugar
1 tsp. salt
1/8 tsp. pepper
3 Tbsp. dried minced onion
3 Tbsp. grated Parmesan cheese
4 c. all-purpose flour
1/2 c. cornmeal
cornmeal
milk
poppy seeds (optional)

In a large mixing bowl, dissolve yeast in warm water. Stir in 1/2 tsp. sugar; let stand until foamy, 5 to 10 minutes.

In a small saucepan, combine 3/4 c. milk, mashed potatoes, margarine, 1 Tbsp. sugar, salt and pepper. Cook and stir over medium heat until mixture is warm (margarine may not be melted). Remove from heat. Stir in dried onion and Parmesan cheese; let stand for 5 minutes.

Stir mashed potato mixture into yeast mixture. At low speed of an electric mixer or by hand, beat in 1 1/2 c. of the flour and 1/2 c. cornmeal until well blended.

At medium speed, beat for 2 minutes. By hand, gradually add flour to form a stiff dough. On a floured surface, knead until smooth and elastic, 5 to 8 minutes.

Place in a lightly greased bowl; turn to coat all surfaces. Cover with plastic wrap, then a towel and let rise in a warm place, free from drafts, until doubled, about 1 hour.

Punch down dough. Divide into three equal portions. Roll and stretch each portion to form 14-inch long ropes. Cover with a towel and let rest for 5 minutes (ropes may shrink slightly).

Grease a baking sheet. Sprinkle with cornmeal. Gently place ropes side-by-side diagonally on baking sheet. Loosely braid, pinching ends to seal, then tuck ends under the braid. Cover and let rise in a warm place until almost doubled, about 30 minutes. Brush top with milk, and if desired, sprinkle with poppy seeds.

Bake in middle of a preheated 375 degree oven for 30 to 35 minutes or until braid sounds hollow when tapped. If needed to prevent overbrowning, cover top loosely with foil after 20 minutes of baking. Transfer braid to a wire rack and cool.

Yield: one 14-inch braid

MAIDA HEATTER'S SWEET POTATO POUND CAKE

2/3 c. salted peanuts
2 1/2 c. mashed, canned, or baked sweet potatoes
3 c. all-purpose flour, sifted
2 tsp. double-acting baking powder
1 tsp. baking soda
1 tsp. cinnamon
3/4 tsp. nutmeg
1/4 tsp. salt
8 oz. (2 sticks) unsalted butter
1 tsp. vanilla extract
1 c. granulated sugar
1 c. light brown sugar, firmly packed
4 large eggs

Adjust a rack one third up from the bottom of the oven and preheat the oven to 350 degrees.

Butter a 10-inch Bundt pan (or any other tube pan with a design and a 14-cup capacity), even if it has a non-stick finish.

Place the peanuts in the bowl of a food processor fitted with the metal chopping blade and process them for about 5 seconds until they are fine but uneven, or chop/grind them any other way.

Place peanuts in the buttered pan (use your fingertips to sprinkle them on the center tube), rotate and tilt the pan to coat all parts of it, then invert the pan over paper for excess nuts to fall out. Do not tap the pan — you want as heavy a coating of nuts as will hold. About half the nuts that fall onto the paper should be sprinkled back over the bottom of the pan to make a heavy layer. The remaining nuts should be set aside to be sprinkled over the top of the cake.

If you are using canned sweet potatoes or yams, pour them into a strainer to drain off all the syrup. In a food processor fitted with metal chopping blade, process half of the sweet potatoes at a time; it will be necessary to stop the machine frequently and scrape the sides of the bowl with a rubber spatula. Do not add any liquid; the sweet potatoes should be dry. Or they can be mashed in a large bowl with a potato masher. They must be perfectly smooth. Set aside.

Sift together the flour, baking powder, baking soda, cinnamon, nutmeg and salt and set aside.

In a large bowl of an electric mixer, beat the butter until soft. Add the vanilla and both sugars and beat until mixed. Beat in the eggs 1 at a time (the mixture will appear curdled but it will be all right). Add the mashed potatoes and beat to mix. Then, on low speed, add the sifted dry ingredients and beat until incorporated, scraping the bowl as necessary with a rubber spatula.

Turn the batter into the prepared pan. Smooth the top. Sprinkle with reserved chopped peanuts.

Bake for 1 hour and 15 minutes until a cake tester comes out dry and clean.

Let the cake stand in the pan for 15 minutes. Then remove it to the serving plate or to a rack as follows. To remove it to the plate, just cover the pan with the plate, hold them together and turn them both over and remove the pan.

To transfer the cake to a rack first, cover the top of the cake pan with a 12-inch square of aluminum foil, fold down the sides, cover with a rack, hold them together and turn everything over, and remove the pan (this keeps the loose nuts from flying around). Let stand until cool and then transfer to a serving plate or board.

Yield: 16 servings

Mary Hille McCoy
Monterey, VA

SWEET POTATO TEA CAKES

1 1/2 c. flour
1/2 tsp. baking soda
1/2 tsp. salt
1 1/2 tsp. cinnamon
1 c. granulated sugar
1 c. cooked, mashed sweet potato
2 eggs, beaten
2/3 c. melted margarine
1/2 c. shredded coconut
1/2 c. seedless raisins
1/2 c. walnuts

Place all dry ingredients in mixing bowl and make a well in center, add all other ingredients. Stir carefully just enough to moisten. Bake in loaf pan for 1 hour at 350 degrees. Cool before slicing.

Yield: 1 loaf

Mary Hille McCoy
Monterey, VA

MORAVIAN SUGAR CAKE

1 pkg. dry yeast
1/2 c. warm water
1 c. sugar
4 Tbsp. butter
1/2 c. shortening
1 tsp. salt
1 c. hot dry mashed potatoes
1 c. potato water
2 eggs, well beaten
5 c. flour

Combine yeast and 1/2 cup warm water. Cream together the sugar, butter, shortening and salt. Combine with yeast and water. Add the potatoes and potato water. Let rise 1/2 hour. Add eggs and flour. Let rise until double in size (4 to 5 hours or overnight). Spread in two 9 X 13 pans. Dot with butter and brown sugar pressed into dough. Sprinkle liberally with cinnamon. Bake at 350 degrees about 20 minutes.

Yield: 48 servings

Mary Ann Johnson
Richmond, VA

CARBOHYDRATES

The potato has been criticized for being "just a starch." There's a lot more to potatoes, of course, but the carbohydrates in potatoes are the most common form of complex carbohydrates and as such are important to a good diet. Carbohydrates are the body's primary source of fuel for energy. Experts say at least 50% of our daily body fuel should come from carbohydrates. Carbohydrates are of serveral types. Sugars are the most basic carbohydrates, the building blocks of complex carbohydrates. Complex carbohydrates are longer chains of sugars, such as starches and fiber.

Contrary to popular belief, gram for gram, carbohydrates have no more calories than protein and less than half that of fat. In fact, potatoes are virtually fat-free.

CHOCOLATE POTATO CAKE

3/4 c. butter or margarine, softened
1 1/2 c. sugar
4 eggs, separated
1 c. hot riced potatoes
1 1/2 c. sifted all purpose flour
2 tsp. baking powder
1/2 tsp. salt
1/2 c. cocoa
1 tsp. ground cinnamon
1/2 tsp. ground nutmeg
1/4 tsp. ground cloves
1/2 c. milk
1 tsp. vanilla extract
1 c. nuts, chopped
Fluffy White Frosting*

Cream butter and 1 c. sugar until light. Add egg yolks and beat well. Add potato and mix thoroughly. Add sifted dry ingredients alternately with milk, beating until smooth. Add vanilla and nuts. Beat egg whites until stiff but not dry. Gradually add remaining sugar, beating until very stiff. Fold into first mixture. Pour into pan (13 X 9), lined in the bottom with wax paper. Bake in preheated oven of 350 degrees for about 45 minutes. Cool and frost with fluffy white frosting.

*Fluffy White Frosting:

2 egg whites
1 1/2 c. sugar
1/2 tsp. salt
1/3 c. water
2 tsp. light corn syrup
1 tsp. vanilla extract

In top of small double boiler, combine egg whites, sugar, salt, water, and syrup. Put over boiling water and beat well with rotary beater or electric beater for 7 minutes or until mixture will stand in stiff peaks. Fold in vanilla extract.

Yield: 16 servings

RAW SWEET POTATO PUDDING

2 c. grated sweet potato
1 c. sugar
1 c. milk
2 eggs, beaten
1/2 c. raisins (golden raisins, preferable)
1/2 tsp. nutmeg
1/2 tsp. salt
1/2 stick butter, melted
1/2 c. coconut (optional)
1 tsp. vanilla

Mix all of the above together. Bake at 350 degrees for 45-60 minutes. Serve warm with dollop of whipped cream. Sprinkle with nutmeg.

Yield: 4-6 servings

Martha Chamberlain
Springfield, VA

POTATO CHIP COOKIES

1 lb. margarine
1 c. sugar
2 tsp. vanilla
3 1/2 c. plain flour
1 c. crushed potato chips

Cream margarine and sugar. Add remaining ingredients and mix well. Roll into balls the size desired and flatten with fork on ungreased cookie sheet. Bake at 350 degrees for 12-15 minutes.

Yield: 5 doz. (depending on size)

Norlee Smith
Alexandria, VA

STEAMED CARROT PUDDING

1 egg
1 c. ground raw carrots
1 c. ground raw potatoes
2 c. raisins
3/4 c. whole wheat flour
1/4 c. bread crumbs
1/2 c. margarine, melted
1/3 c. brown sugar
1/3 c. granulated sugar
1 1/2 tsp. baking powder
1 tsp. ground cinnamon
1/2 tsp. ground nutmeg
1/2 tsp. ground cloves
1/2 tsp. ground allspice
1/2 tsp. salt
Pinch baking soda

Beat egg in a large mixing bowl. Add all other ingredients and mix well. Fill two or three greased cans to within two-thirds of top. (Recycled soup or fruit cans work well.) Cover cans with foil and steam for 2 1/2 hrs. (A spaghetti cooker with its rack for a steamer can be used.) Serve with hot grape sauce.

CHAFF GRAPE SAUCE

1/4 c. sugar
pinch salt
2 Tbsp. cornstarch
2 c. grape juice
1 Tbsp. lemon juice

Mix dry ingredients in saucepan, add grape juice and stir until blended. Cook over medium heat, stirring constantly until sauce boils and thickens. Remove from heat. Add lemon juice. Serve hot or cold. This sauce may be stored in the refrigerator and reheated.

Yield: 8-10 servings

Joanne Milkereit
Charleston, SC

SWEET POTATO POUND CAKE

1/2 c. shortening
1/2 c. butter or margarine, softened
2 c. sugar
6 eggs
3 c. all-purpose flour
1/2 tsp. salt
1/4 tsp. baking soda
1 tsp. baking powder
1 c. buttermilk
1 c. cooked puréed sweet potatoes
1/2 tsp. almond extract
1/4 tsp. coconut extract
1/4 c. slivered almonds, toasted & finely chopped
1/4 c. flaked coconut

Cream shortening and butter; add sugar, beating well. Add eggs, one at a time, beating after each addition. Combine next 4 ingredients, stirring well; add to creamed mixture alternately with buttermilk, beginning and ending with flour mixture. Stir in sweet potatoes and flavorings.

Grease and flour a 10-inch tube pan; sprinkle almonds and coconut over bottom. Pour batter into pan; bake at 350 degrees for 1 hour and 15 minutes. Cool 10 minutes; remove from pan.

Yield: 1 10-inch cake

Sweet potatoes
"They have them sown with ajes, which are certain slips which they plant, and at the foot of them grow some roots like carrots, which serve as bread and they grate them, knead them and make bread of them. Afterwards they again plant the same slip in another place and it again produces four or five of these roots, which are savoury and have the exact taste of chestnuts."
-Christopher Columbus, 1492

SWEET POTATO-PECAN PIE

1 c. cooked, mashed sweet potato
1 Tbsp butter, softened
1/4 c. firmly packed light brown sugar
1 Tbsp. vanilla extract
1/4 tsp. ground cinnamon
1/8 tsp. ground nutmeg
1/8 tsp. ground allspice
1/4 tsp. salt
1/2 beaten egg
2 Tbsp. sugar
1 Tbsp. whipping cream
pastry (recipe follows)*
1/2 c. pecans, chopped
3/4 c. sugar
2 eggs
3/4 c. dark corn syrup
1 1/2 Tbsp butter, melted
pinch of salt
pinch of ground cinnamon
2 tsp. vanilla extract
whipped cream to top pie

Combine first 11 ingredients; beat at medium speed of an electric mixer until smooth. Spread on bottom of pastry * shell; sprinkle with pecans.

Combine next 7 ingredients, beating well. Pour over pecans. Bake at 300 degrees for 1 1/2 hours. Cool. Top each slice with dollop of whipped cream.

Yield: 1 9-inch pie

*PASTRY:

3 Tbsp. butter, softened
2 Tbsp. sugar
1/2 beaten egg
2 Tbsp. milk

1 c. all-purpose flour

Cream butter and sugar, beating until light and fluffy. Add egg and milk; beat about 2 minutes. Add flour, stirring just until ingredients are moistened. Refrigerate dough at least 1 hour.

Roll dough out to a 14-inch circle on lightly floured wax paper. Invert pastry on lightly floured wax paper. Invert pastry and wax paper onto a deep-dish 9-inch pie plate. Carefully remove wax paper, and press pastry into pie plate. (Dough will be soft and fragile.)

Yield: 1 pie crust

SWEET POTATO MERINGUE PIE

1 1/4 c. cooked, mashed sweet potatoes
2/3 c. sugar
1/2 c. evaporated milk
1/2 c. flaked coconut
1/4 c. plus 2 Tbsp. butter, melted
1/2 tsp. lemon extract
2 eggs, separated
1 unbaked 9-inch pie shell
1/4 c. sugar
1/2 tsp. vanilla extract

Combine first 6 ingredients and egg yolks, mixing well. Spoon mixture into pastry shell. Bake at 350 degrees for 40 to 45 minutes or until knife inserted in center comes out clean.

Beat egg whites (at room temperature) until foamy. Gradually add 1/4 c. sugar, 1 Tbsp. at a time, and vanilla, beating until stiff peaks form. Spread meringue over filling, sealing to edge of pastry. Bake at 400 degrees for 10 minutes or until meringue is golden brown.

Yield: 1 9-inch pie

POTATO FLOUR SPONGE CAKE

4 egg whites
4 egg yolks
3/4 c. sugar
1/2 Tbsp. lemon juice
1/2 c. potato flour
1 tsp. baking powder
1/4 tsp. salt

Measure all ingredients. Sift sugar through fine sifter one to four times before measuring. Sift flour once before measuring. Beat egg whites until stiff but not dry and beat in gradually 1 Tbsp. sugar for each egg white and set aside. Beat egg yolks with same beater until thick and lemon-colored. Beat in remaining sugar. Combine yolks and whites. Mix in remaining dry ingredients. Do not beat after adding flour, to avoid breaking air bubbles. Bake in ungreased layer cake pans (2 pans) at 350 degrees for 30 minutes.

Yield: 8-10 servings

Ruth Smith Newell

FASTNACHT KARTOFFEL KUCHEN
Potato Cake

2 large potatoes, pared
2 eggs
1 c. sugar
1 tsp. salt
1/4 tsp. nutmeg
1/2 c. shortening
1 yeast cake, softened in 1/2 c. warm water
flour

Boil potatoes in enough water to cover them. Drain, saving potato water. Mash potatoes and beat well. Measure potato water and add more water, if necessary to make 1 1/2 pts. Combine with remaining ingredients, including potatoes, using enough flour to make a rather stiff batter. Cover and let rise in a warm place until morning. Knead in the morning, adding as much flour as is necessary to make a stiff dough. Let rise again. Spread on well greased pans and when light, or risen again, (about 1 hour & 15 minutes) brush melted butter over top. Bake at 400 degrees for approximately 20 minutes. Sprinkle with Streusel*.

Yield: 4 9-inch cakes

*Streusel:

1/2 c. sugar
1 tsp. cinnamon
1/4 c. sifted flour
3 Tbsp. soft butter
few drops vanilla
3 Tbsp. chopped nuts, optional

Mix thoroughly sugar, cinnamon and flour. Rub in butter, working it with a fork to form into "crumbs". Add vanilla and nuts, if desired. Sprinkle on top of coffee cakes after removing from oven.

Yield: topping for 2 coffee cakes

Ruth Smith Newell

BERKS COUNTY POTATO CUSTARD PIE

1 med. potato
2 Tbsp. butter
3/4 c. sugar
1/8 tsp. salt
2 eggs, separated
1/2 c. milk
juice & grated rind of 1/2 lemon

Boil potato and mash. Add butter, sugar and salt; stir to a creamy consistency. Cool and add beaten egg yolks, milk, lemon juice and rind. Mix together well and fold in stiffly-beaten egg whites. Pour into unbaked 9-inch pie shell. Bake in 400 degree oven for 25 minutes.

Yield: 1 9-inch pie

Ruth Smith Newell

139

OLD-FASHIONED CHOCOLATE CAKE

2 c. all-purpose flour
2 c. sugar
1 c. unseasoned mashed potatoes, room temperature
3/4 c. milk
4 oz. semisweet chocolate, melted and cooled
3 eggs
1/3 c. butter, softened
1 1/4 tsp. baking soda
1 tsp. salt
1 tsp. vanilla extract
1/2 tsp. baking powder
chocolate frosting*
chopped nuts (optional)

Grease and lightly flour a 13 X 9-inch baking pan.

In a large mixing bowl at low speed, beat flour, sugar, mashed potatoes, milk, chocolate, eggs, butter, baking soda, salt, vanilla and baking powder for 30 seconds, scraping sides frequently. Increase speed to high and beat for 3 minutes, scraping bowl occasionally. Pour into pan.

Bake at 350 degrees for 40 to 45 minutes or until top springs back when lightly pressed and a wooden pick inserted in center comes out clean. Cool on wire rack for 10 minutes. If desired, invert cake onto a wire rack. Cool completely.

Top with Chocolate Frosting and nuts if desired.

Yield: 12-15 servings

*CHOCOLATE FROSTING

1/3 c. butter, softened
3 oz. unsweetened chocolate, melted
3 1/2 c. powdered sugar
4-6 Tbsp. milk or half-and-half
1 tsp. vanilla extract
dash of salt

In a small mixing bowl at medium speed, beat butter and chocolate until smooth.

At low speed, beat in powdered sugar. Beat in 4 Tbsp. milk, vanilla and salt until smooth, adding additional milk if needed, or until spreading consistency.

Frost Old-Fashioned Chocolate Cake

Yield: 2 cups

> *A potato field produces more nutrition more reliably and with less labor than the same field planted in grain.*

SWEET POTATO PIE

1/2 c. brown sugar
1 Tbsp. flour
1/2 tsp. salt
1 tsp. cinnamon
1/2 tsp. nutmeg
1/2 tsp. ginger
1/4 tsp. cloves
1 1/2 c. cooked, mashed sweet potatoes
1 1/2 c. milk
1 egg, beaten
2 Tbsp. butter

Mix all of the above together and pour into an unbaked pie shell. Bake at 450 degrees for 15 minutes or until brown. Decrease heat to 350 degrees and bake until done or about 30 minutes.

Yield: 6-8 servings

Hilda Reeh
Needville, TX

VEGETARIAN CAKE

2 c. all-purpose flour
3 tsp. baking powder
1 1/2 tsp. ground cinnamon
1 1/2 tsp. ground allspice
3/4 tsp. baking soda
1/4 tsp. salt
1 1/2 c. peeled, shredded apples
1 1/2 c. peeled, shredded carrots
1 1/2 c. peeled, shredded potatoes
3/4 c. currants
3/4 c. raisins
3/4 c. chopped walnuts
1 Tbsp. grated orange peel
1 1/2 c. packed brown sugar
3/4 c. margarine, softened
3 eggs
2 Tbsp. light molasses

Generously grease and flour a 10-inch fluted tube pan. Onto waxed paper, sift flour, baking powder, cinnamon, allspice, baking soda and salt; set aside.

In a medium bowl, stir apples, carrots, potatoes, currants, raisins, nuts and orange peel; set aside.

In a large mixing bowl at medium speed, beat brown sugar and butter until fluffy. Add eggs and molasses and beat until well blended. At low speed, beat in dry ingredients until moistened. Gradually add vegetable mixture and beat in dry ingredients until well blended. Spoon into pan. Bake at 350 degrees for 60 minutes or until a wooden pick inserted 1 inch from outer edge comes out clean and cake pulls away from pan. Cool on a wire rack for 10 minutes; remove cake from pan and cool completely.

Cover and store in the refrigerator. May be served with a Vanilla Glaze*, if desired. This cake is best served the second day. Slice cake with a sharp knife.

Yield: 12-15 servings

*VANILLA GLAZE

This is an all-purpose glaze.

2 c. sifted powdered sugar
1/4 c. half-and-half
1 Tbsp. butter, softened
1/2 tsp. vanilla extract

In a small mixing bowl at medium speed, beat powdered sugar, half-and-half, butter and vanilla until smooth and creamy.

Yield: 3/4 cup

COCONUT POTATO COOKIES

1/3 c. butter or margarine
1 c. sugar
1 egg
1 tsp. coconut flavoring
1 pkg. buttermilk biscuit mix (5 oz.)
1 pkg. instant potato flakes (2 or 2 3/4 oz.)

Cream butter and sugar. Add egg, biscuit mix, potato flakes, and flavoring. Mix thoroughly.

Roll into balls about an inch in diameter. Bake on ungreased cookie sheet at 350 degrees for 10 minutes or until light brown.

Yield: 3 1/2 doz.

Sue Byrne
Lowry, VA

APRICOT SCONES

1/2 c. snipped dried apricots
hot tap water
1 1/2 c. all-purpose flour
1/4 c. sugar
1 1/2 tsp. baking powder
1/2 tsp. salt
1/8 tsp. ground cinnamon
1/3 c. butter, chilled
3/4 c. unseasoned mashed potatoes
1 egg
3 Tbsp. milk
1 Tbsp. sliced almonds
1 tsp. sugar

Lightly grease a baking sheet.

Cover apricots with water and let stand for 10 minutes.

Meanwhile, in a large bowl, combine flour, 1/4 c. sugar, baking powder, salt and cinnamon. With a pastry blender or two knives, cut in butter until mixture resembles coarse crumbs. Thoroughly drain apricots. Stir apricots and mashed potatoes into flour mixture.

In a small bowl, whisk together egg and milk; set 1/2 Tbsp. of the mixture aside. Stir remaining mixture into flour mixture just until dry ingredients are moistened. Knead 6 to 8 times to form a ball. Place on baking sheet. Flatten into a 7-inch circle. With a floured knife, cut into six wedges, but do not separate.

Brush top with reserved egg-milk mixture. Sprinkle with almonds and 1 tsp. sugar.

Bake at 400 degrees for 22 to 24 minutes or until lightly browned. Serve immediately with butter and jam or honey.

Yield: 6 servings

WHITE POTATO PIE

2 c. mashed potatoes
3 eggs, separated
1 1/2 c. white sugar
1 tsp. lemon juice
1/2 c. butter
2 c. milk
1 pie crust

Add sugar to potatoes and butter. Beat egg yolks a little, add milk and lemon. Mix well. Beat egg whites till stiff and fold into potatoes. Pour into pie crust and bake at 450 degrees for 15 minutes. Then bake at 350 degrees until the center is set (knife blade comes out clean).

Yield: 6-8 servings

Margaret Briscoe
Galena, MD

CHOCOLATE FRENCH CREAM

1 lb. potatoes, peeled and cooked
5 oz. unsweetened chocolate, melted
3/4 c. soft butter
1 1/2 c. sugar
1 tsp. vanilla
1 tsp. instant coffee
2 egg yolks

Work butter until it is creamy, gradually work in sugar until smooth. Add vanilla and instant coffee. Add egg yolks and beat hard; add the melted chocolate and beat hard. Put potatoes through sieve or a potato ricer. Add hot potato to the chocolate mixture and mix well. Spoon into dish and chill overnight. Serve with whipped cream.

Yield: 4-6 servings

POTATO CANDY I

1 potato
confectioners' sugar
1 tsp. vanilla
peanut butter

Peel one small potato and cook until tender. Drain and mash.
Add enough confectioners' sugar to make a stiff dough. Flavor
with vanilla (about 1 teaspoon).

Flour a board very slightly with sifted confectioners' sugar.
Knead the dough until it can be rolled out to about the consistency of pie crust. Spread with peanut butter. Roll as for jelly
roll or cinnamon rolls. Cut cross-wise, chill and serve.

Yield: 8-12 pieces

Nancy H. West
Dumfries, VA

POTATO CANDY II

1 medium potato
2 tsp. butter
4 oz. coconut
1 tsp. vanilla
1 lb. confectioners' sugar
2 squares bitter chocolate, melted

Boil potato until tender, remove skin and mash potato fine.
Discard skin. Add to the mashed potato, butter, coconut, vanilla
and powdered sugar, mixing well after each addition. Beat mixture until creamy. Put about one inch thick into buttered pan.
Let stand until hardened. Pour melted chocolate over potato
mixture. Put into refrigerator about 2 hours. Cut into squares.

Yield: 12-15 pieces

Mrs. Gertrude Humphrey
Alexandria, VA

Cooking
for a Crowd
&
Hunger Awareness
Meals

notes

Many of our supporting churches and organizations raise money for the Society of St. Andrew by serving potato meals. It has been requested that a section on cooking for a crowd be included in our cookbook. Recipes follow that are favorites of Dorothy Schminkey of Arlington, VA that she so graciously adapted for a crowd.

SAVORY POTATO SOUP

2 lbs. onions, chopped
1 lb. oleo
1 lb. celery, chopped
1 stalk celery, diced
7 1/2 lbs. peeled potatoes, diced
4 gals. water
3 Tbsp. salt
1 Tbsp. pepper
1 c. flour
2 Tbsp. parsley flakes

Sauté the onions in the melted oleo until light brown. Remove fat and reserve.

Cook potatoes and celery slowly in water with salt, pepper and onions until potatoes are reduced to pulp. Purée or mash.

Blend reserved oleo (fat) and flour, add to soup and boil until slightly thickened. Add parsley flakes and serve.

Yield: 50 servings

CREAM OF POTATO SOUP

12 lbs. peeled potatoes, diced
1/2 lb. onions, chopped
9 qts. water

Cook the above until the potatoes are soft. Purée or mash without draining.

White Sauce:
1 lb. oleo
1 c. flour
2 tsp. pepper
5 Tbsp. salt
9 qts. hot milk
3 Tbsp. parsley flakes

Melt oleo in large pot. Blend in flour, pepper and salt. When well blended, add milk. When sauce is thickened add white sauce to the potato mixture and bring to a boil. Add parsley flakes and serve.

Yield: 50 servings

BAKED POTATO BAR

50 potatoes, wrapped in foil and baked

2 lbs. butter
1 1/2 qts. sour cream
2 lbs. cheese, shredded
3 lbs. Velveeta cheese, melted
4 qts. chili with beans
bacon bits
chives

Yield: 50 servings

150

Hunger Awareness Meals

Try one of the hunger awareness meals described below as an eye-opening program for a church or community supper or youth group meeting. Admission to the dinner can be collected to send food to hungry people through the Society of St. Andrew's Potato Project!

Many of us, especially those who have never had the opportunity to travel abroad, do not realize how many people in the world live without things that we consider basic necessities of life: food, clothing, shelter, and education. Hunger awareness meals are unique educational experiences because they illustrate the disparities that exist among the nations of the world by dealing with something important to all of us: our food.

The goal of a hunger awareness meal is to do just what its name implies: raise the awareness of the participants that hunger is an unwelcome but common part of the life of much of the world's family. The global hunger awareness meal which follows has been adapted from **Hunger Awareness Dinners** by Aileen Van Beilen, Herald Press, Scottsdale, PA., 1978 (used by permission).

Global Hunger Awareness Meal

Overview:

In the global hunger awareness meal, participants are divided into 5 groups representing five regions: North America, Europe, Latin America, Africa, and Asia. The meal each participant receives represents the average calories and protein consumption for a meal among the people who are living in that region. Because of the nature of the world's food distribution, some people will receive more than they can eat, but a majority of the people will receive very little to eat. This experience can bring about some very strong feelings and emotions, so it is important to allow time for a discussion following the meal to work out those feelings.

Set-up for the Meal:

Planning for the meal should begin well in advance since set-up, meal preparation, and serving can take some time. See "Global Hunger Awareness Meal Information Table" for population percentages, menus, and table preparations.

It is important that participants do not know the true nature of the meal. Perhaps just promote the meal as an international dinner followed by a short program. Be sure to keep participants away from the dining area until meal time. Then just before the meal, have participants draw a colored ticket from a basket or bag to determine where they will sit. Use the population percentages from the information table to determine how many people to put at each table (Multiply the number of people attending the meal by the percentage for each region. For example, 40 people X 5% = 2 people to sit at the North American table.) Each table or area should have a colored placard which states the region it represents and corresponds to the tickets.

Tables are set up according to the type of meal that region will receive. For example, the North American table should be very elegant, with a white tablecloth, candles, flowers, and even a waiter or waitress to bring them their meal. The

European table has a simpler look, and the food is served family style. The Asians, on the other hand, do not even have a table; they will sit on the floor in a corner of the room. (Don't forget to stress during the discussion time, though, that not all Americans are so well fed and that not all Asians have such meager diets.)

There are no set rules for the meal. Nor are there any right or wrong ways to have the meal proceed. Whatever way the meal proceeds provides fuel for an effective, awareness-building discussion. Have 2-3 people who will take charge of the discussion after the meal. These people, who function as participants/observers, should be particularly aware of what happens during the meal, so they can better facilitate the discussion which follows the meal.

Discussion:

The discussion following the meal is a critical time to process all the feelings of guilt, anger, or frustration that many participants may feel as a result of the experience. The discussion facilitators should start off the discussion by asking questions such as:

How are you feeling? (hungry, guilty, angry)
What bothered you about this meal?
How is this like/unlike real life?
There was enough food for everyone here.
How could things have happened differently so that everyone could be fed?

The facilitators should try to draw responses from all of the participants. They should watch for those who might over-personalize the activity. Those who sit at the North American table are particularly prone to this. They fear that their lack of sharing or their sharing in a condescending manner might indicate that they are selfish or condescending people. They need to be reassured that anyone at the table could have acted similarly. They, in a sense, represent all of us, since we are all North Americans.

To close the discussion, it is important to stress the many things that we can do to help our global brothers and sisters. Have materials on hand which provide ideas for both volunteer support and financial support.

Global Hunger Awareness Meal Information Table

North America (5% of the people): Serve sliced ham, baked or scalloped potatoes, hot vegetable, roll, green salad, pie w/ topping, coffee, tea, milk, cream, sugar, salt, butter, etc. Set the tables with linen tablecloths, napkins w/holders, crystal goblets, silver candlesticks w/red candles (lit), salad bowls, bread & butter plates, dinner plates, etc., and a showy center-piece.

Europe (15% of the people): Serve vegetable soup, open-faced meat & cheese sandwich, fried sliced potatoes, fresh fruit, tea, water. Set each table with a white cloth tablecloth, purple placemats, simple attractive setting of dishes & silverware (bowl, small plate, cup, saucer, usual silverware) and a simple fresh flower centerpiece.

Latin America (10% of the people): Serve rice (3/4 c. each), garbanzo beans, chicken broth, tomato juice (poured or in pitcher), water, coffee. Serve on tables with no tablecloth using blue placemats, very simple dishes —(bowl, spoon, glass, cup, no saucer).

Africa (10% of the people): Serve mashed potatoes, bread, water and tea. Serve on tables with no tablecloth using green paper placemats, very simple bowl, cup & spoon.

Asia (60% of the people): Serve rice and tea. Serve on floor, very simple bowl, cup & spoon.

(Note: Actual population percentages are as follows: North America - 6%, Europe - 16%, Latin America - 8%, Africa - 12%, Asia - 58%. Statistics from Population Reference Bureau, Washington, D.C.)

A Variation:
Domestic Hunger Awareness Meal

It is easy to adapt the global hunger awareness meal to a more domestic setting. This meal would be effective for a group which has hosted global meals before or has been studying domestic hunger and poverty issues. For general planning and discussion, follow the instructions for the global hunger awareness meal.

The domestic meal has 6 table locations representing the following: holiday dinner, family dinner, fast food dinner, low-cost dinner, soup kitchen/shelter dinner, and dinner "on the streets."

1. Holiday Dinner

Serve lots of food family style with all the trimmings, centerpiece, music, etc. Use the menu and table setting information for the North American table from the "Global Hunger Awareness Meal Information Table."

2. Family Dinner

Serve a meal that might be considered a typical family meal. Menu suggestion: spaghetti, salad, garlic bread, cake, iced tea, and coffee.

3. Fast Food Dinner

Menu suggestion: pizza and soda or some other kind of fast food meal.

4. Low-Cost Dinner

Many people on limited income budgets or government assistance must stretch food dollars, especially at the end of the month when money often runs out. Low-cost meals often stress high carbohydrate content and include very few fresh fruits and vegetables or meats. Menu suggestion: beans or macaroni and cheese, and water (small portions).

5. Soup Kitchen/Shelter Dinner

Menu suggestion: vegetable soup, sandwich, day-old cookies or doughnut, and container of milk or coffee.

6. Dinner "On the Streets"

This meal would consist of food that might be obtained by someone who is homeless and is living on the streets. There should be no table for this meal. Menu suggestion: part of a sandwich, a stale roll, and a brown banana.

The table of population statistics which follows presents individual yearly income percentages for individuals over age 14 in the United States. Use this table as a guideline in determining the population breakdown for each table in the domestic meal.

Yearly income percentages

  4% Wealthy (earning $50,000 and above)
11% Upper Middle (earning $30,000 - $49,999)
18% Middle (earning $17,500 - $29,999)
24% Lower Middle (earning $8,500 - $17,499)
36% Poor, with income (earning $8499 and below)
  7% Poor, without income
(Population Reference Bureau, Washington, D.C.)

Note: When interpreting these statistics, consider that these figures represent an average for the entire country, and do not take into consideration high and low cost-of-living areas, multiple family households, and family size.

As an additional guideline for your planning, note that 1989 figures estimate the homeless population in the United States at 1% of the population, or 3 million people, on any given night. (National Coalition for the Homeless, Washington, D.C.)

Index

Index

Side Dishes (cont.)

Main Dishes

Breads & Desserts

Cooking For A Crowd
&
Hunger Awareness Meals

For Additional Copies

Please send me_____copies of **"Please Pass the Potatoes, Appeeling Recipes from the Society of St. Andrew "**. Please include $7.50 per copy ordered. My payment of $_____ is enclosed. For large order discounts call 1-800-333-4597.

(Please Print)
Name_____

Address_____

City_____

State _____ Zip _____ Phone_____

Mail to: Society of St. Andrew
P.O. Box 329
Big Island, VA 24526

Additional Information

Please send me additional information on the ministries of the Society of St. Andrew. I am particularly interested in:

☐ Potato Project   ☐ Harvest of Hope

☐ Gleaning Network   ☐ International

☐ All of the ministries

(Please Print)
Name_____

Address_____

City_____

State_____ Zip_____ Phone_____

Return form to: **Society of St. Andrew**
                          P.O. Box 329
                          Big Island, VA 24526
                          1-800-333-4597